MASTERING
CIVILITY

MASTERING CIVILITY

A Manifesto for the Workplace

CHRISTINE PORATH

GRAND CENTRAL
PUBLISHING

NEW YORK   BOSTON

Grand Central Publishing
Hachette Book Group
1290 Avenue of the Americas
New York, NY 10104
grandcentralpublishing.com
twitter.com/grandcentralpub

First Edition: December 2016

Grand Central Publishing is a division of Hachette Book Group, Inc.
The Grand Central Publishing name and logo is a trademark of Hachette Book Group, Inc.

The publisher is not responsible for websites (or their content) that are not owned by the publisher.

The Hachette Speakers Bureau provides a wide range of authors for speaking events. To find out more, go to www.hachettespeakersbureau.com or call (866) 376-6591.

Thermometer photo created by Mike Porath, illustrated by Valeria Khislavsky

CYCLE TO CIVILITY is a registered trademark owned by Christine Porath.

Who's (Civil) In Your Group? Christine Porath © 2015

SERVE Model © 2001, CFA Properties, Inc., Chick-fil-A® is a registered trademark of CFA Properties, Inc. Used with permission. All Rights Reserved.

Library of Congress Cataloging-in-Publication Data

Names: Porath, Christine Lynne, author.
Title: Mastering civility : a manifesto for the workplace / Christine Porath.
Description: First edition. | New York, NY : Grand Central Publishing, [2016] | Includes bibliographical references and index.
Identifiers: LCCN 2016028809| ISBN 9781455568987 (hardcover) | ISBN 9781478967118 (audio download) | ISBN 9781455568994 (e-book)
Subjects: LCSH: Employee morale. | Courtesy in the workplace. | Interpersonal relations. | Work environment. | Organizational behavior.
Classification: LCC HF5549.5.M6 P67 2016 | DDC 650.1/3—dc23 LC record available at https://lccn.loc.gov/2016028809

ISBNs: 978-1-4555-6898-7 (hardcover), 978-1-4789-6711-8 (audiobook downloadable), 978-1-4555-6899-4 (ebook), 978-1-4789-4789-9 (international)

Printed in the United States of America

LSC-C

10 9 8 7 6 5 4 3 2 1

For Mom and Dad

Contents

Contents

PART IV: Lift Yourself: Handling Incivility if *You're* the Target

MASTERING
CIVILITY

Introduction

After delivering a talk at the Department of Labor about overcoming incivility and creating a thriving environment, I stepped into an elevator with some senior executives from the office of the secretary of labor and a few others. One woman standing next to me introduced herself; she had attended my talk and wanted to tell me about an extremely unpleasant problem she was having with an uncivil boss. I listened as she described the situation. She was careful not to name names, but it became increasingly obvious that the uncivil offender was a leader in the organization, someone in the chain between her and the deputy. All other conversation in the elevator had stopped; those around us awkwardly stared off into space or kept their eyes glued to the floor, but they *all* were listening.

"What should I do?" this woman asked. "I'm at wits' end. How do I handle this uncivil person I have to work with?"

Then, the elevator door opened, and as we all got out, this woman stuck by my side. Stress was eating away at her; I could see it. As we walked down the hallway to the deputy's office, I offered some general recommendations, telling her to focus on taking care of herself, that ultimately it wasn't worth being pulled off track by him. I suggested she spend time with people and activities that would inspire or elevate her. This woman nodded, but she was clearly unsatisfied with my advice. "Look," she said by way of good-bye as I turned to walk into a meeting, "I'm totally stuck. I don't want to leave my job; I have so much invested here. I work hard and I want better, not just for me but for everyone. I just don't know how to get it."

I felt this woman's pain, because I had been there myself. At the beginning of my career, I scored what I thought was my dream job, helping a global athletic brand launch a sports academy. As I soon discovered, I had walked into an uncivil work culture where bullying, rudeness, and other forms of incivility ran rampant. The actions of a narcissistic, dictatorial boss trickled down through the ranks. Employees felt disconnected and disengaged. Some intentionally sabotaged the organization, stealing supplies and equipment, padding their time cards with hours they hadn't worked and charging personal items to their expense accounts. Many took out their frustrations on others, barking orders at colleagues, making snide remarks to customers, and failing to pitch in like good teammates do. Many talented people left, with some joining competing businesses. I was one of them.

I'd like to say the experience left me unscathed, but that wouldn't be true. I was a strong person (or so I thought); after all, I was a two-sport college athlete at a Division I school. My colleagues were resilient as well—not the type of people who would wilt easily when challenged. Yet many of us were depleted after just a few months of working in a hostile environment. We quickly became husks of our former selves.

After this experience, and watching as my loved ones faced uncivil behaviors over the years, I decided to dedicate my professional life to studying incivility in the workplace and to helping build more positive cultures where people can thrive. Wanting to demonstrate to the world that the way people treat one another at work *matters*, I set out to show what leaders and organizations lose financially when they allow rudeness to run rampant. I believed there was a moral element to it—people should treat one another better—but I also knew that for most organizations, money talks, and I wanted to show that incivility hits bottom lines hard. Given how much time we spend at work, and how closely we connect our identities and happiness to our careers, I thought that we could do better—that we *had* to do better. I wanted to show how creating positive, civil workplaces would be good for people, organizations, and society.

Over the past twenty years, I've researched the experiences of tens of thousands of people across six continents in nearly every industry and type of organization, including start-ups, Fortune 500 giants, nonprofits, and government agencies. I've consulted with scores of companies around the world of every size and variety. And I've discovered that one question defines our professional success more than any other. Just one.

Who do you want to be?

Whether you know it or not, you're answering this question every day through your actions. Consider the following scenarios:

Scenario 1

Kate has no energy because she doesn't feel valued. She isn't motivated because she feels like she's set up to fail. She's frustrated because she wants to succeed, but she feels she can't. She's nasty to her coworkers because she doesn't feel respected. She gives less because she's being held down.

Scenario 2

Kate is energized because she feels valued by others. She's inspired because she feels empowered. She's happy because she feels good about what she's accomplishing. She sparks ideas in others because she's a part of a culture that values sharing. She's proud of her work because she's recognized and rewarded for it. She gives more because she's being lifted up.

The question here is not "Which Kate do you want to be?" That's obvious. The question is "Will you lift Kate up or hold her down?" Whether you're a leader trying to achieve results and enhance a work environment or a professional dealing with bad behavior in your workplace, you can succeed by being someone who gets others to give more. How you treat people means everything—whether they will trust you, build relationships with you, follow you, support you, and work hard for you, or not.

Many leaders know that incivility is costly, but they don't always recognize just how much civility pays or how to make it happen. This book will help. It's a practical guide for leaders seeking to build civil workplaces and for anyone trying to become more effective and influential at work. Just because you're not leading an organization doesn't mean you can't still make it better for everyone. In fact, my research confirms that your kindness, consideration, and respect can have a potent effect, creating a positive dynamic of civility that others will respond to and build on.

Besides my own work, this book presents groundbreaking studies from many of my colleagues as well as examples of civility's power inside and outside the workplace. The book is divided into four parts. In part 1, I'll describe incivility and what I've learned about its costs. I'll detail what civility is and just how much it pays. In part 2, I'll ask, "How are you treating others, and what can you do to increase your influence and effectiveness?" In part 3, I'll present a four-step approach to making your organization more civil. In part 4, I'll conclude by offering the advice that the unfortunate woman in the elevator was seeking: what to do if you're a target of incivility.

After twenty years working in the field, I'm disappointed to report that the incivility problem still hasn't been solved. In fact, it's gotten much worse. All of us desperately need to change this reality, for the sake of people *and* organizations. That's why this isn't just a how-to book; it's a manifesto. Mustering the latest science, I hope to convince and inspire you to work just a little harder to be just a little kinder. I want us *all* to stop sidestepping or resisting civility and to start contributing to it.

As you read this book, I hope you will ask yourself who you want to be. And don't do it just once while you're reading; do it several times a day as you react to all the challenges and victories and surprises and tensions you encounter. How do you want to affect people? What impact do you want to have? Take the advice and science in this book to answer these questions, and make your team, organization, and society just a little bit better.

PART I

The Stakes:
The High Costs of
Incivility and the Potential
Gains of Civility

The next four chapters describe the costs of incivility and the surprising benefits of civility. They also show just how rapidly incivility and civility can spread. How we treat others may seem insignificant, but it has important effects on the people around us and the organizations in which we work.

CHAPTER 1

Clueless

Every action done in company ought to be with some sign of respect to those that are present.

—George Washington

Mike, an executive vice president of an entertainment company, flew to New York to help lay off several people with the general manager (GM) of a firm Mike's company had recently acquired. As Mike broke the difficult news to a loyal employee, he was shocked to see the GM sitting with his feet propped up on the conference table, pecking away on his computer. The GM didn't even bother to glance up from his computer screen, let alone thank his direct report or express his sympathy.

Thoughtless actions such as these leave many of us feeling disrespected at work, creating problems that are getting worse by the year. A quarter of the people surveyed by Christine Pearson, a professor at Thunderbird School of Global Management, and me back in 1998 reported that they were treated rudely at least once a week. When I performed the survey again in 2005, that number had risen to nearly half, and when I repeated it again in 2011, it was more than half.

In the *Civility in America 2016* survey, almost all respondents—95 percent—believed we have a civility problem in America; 74 percent believed it was worse now than it had been a few years ago; and 70 percent believed incivility has reached crisis proportions.[1] By all accounts, incivility has only gotten worse.

As you can probably attest, rude behaviors range widely—from ignoring people, as the GM did, to not listening to intentionally undermining others. One boss said, "If I wanted to know what you thought, I'd ask you"; another told a rookie, "This assignment is crap," in response to his first project. A leader screamed, "You made a mistake!" after an employee overlooked a minor typo in an internal memo. A vice president, upset about the lack of financial information that was not yet available, said over the speakerphone in her car, with other people in it, that "this was kindergarten work."

Other common examples of incivility include walking out of a conversation due to lack of interest or answering calls in the middle of meetings. Some leaders behave uncivilly by

- publicly mocking and belittling people;
- reminding subordinates of their "roles" and lesser titles in the organization;
- teasing direct reports in ways that sting; or
- taking credit for wins, but pointing the finger at others when difficulties arise.

In any of these instances, what matters is not whether people *actually* were disrespected or treated insensitively but whether they *felt* disrespected. Incivility is in the eyes of the recipient. It varies not just by individual but also by culture, generation, gender, industry, and organization. What you consider uncivil may not be the same thing your boss considers uncivil. And guess what. What you think matters *most*!

Interpreting the Trends

So why is incivility getting worse? One factor is globalization—colleagues from one culture sometimes unknowingly behave or speak in ways that colleagues from other cultures find rude. When taking the subway in Japan, for example, it's polite to stand on the platform to the side of a train's doors, patiently waiting as travelers disembark, before moving to the center and stepping onto the train. In China, everybody races for the doors all at once—and it's not considered impolite.

Or consider the experience of my mentor, Ed Lawler, director of the Center for Effective Organizations at the University of Southern California. Years ago, he gave a talk to a group of students in a large auditorium in South Africa. He couldn't figure out why he was putting everyone to sleep. All the students had their heads down the entire time. No eye contact, no friendly nods, no smiles—nothing. Only later did he learn that this gesture—the bowing of the head—signified deference and an immense respect for him.

Another factor is generation. Research conducted by Jean Twenge, professor at San Diego State University, reveals that students are about 30 percent more narcissistic than the average students were twenty-five years ago.[2] If you're excessively focused on yourself, you're going to be that much less concerned about the effects of your behavior on others.

But incivility's causes are more complicated than that. We can also tie our epidemic of rudeness to a general fraying of workplace relationships. Part of this stems from different work arrangements since fewer people work at the office. Even if people choose to work from home, they feel the effects of a bubble. Those who work at a distance report feeling more isolated and less respected at their organization.[3] Books like Robert Putnam's *Bowling Alone* and Marc Dunkelman's *The Vanishing Neighbor* have chronicled the dissolution of communal and civic ties,[4] and based on the work I do, I'd extend that to organizations. In a study I did of twenty thousand mostly white-collar employees across companies and industries, more than half felt stressed and overloaded. In a separate survey, I directly asked respondents why they behave uncivilly. More than half claimed it was because they are overloaded, and more than 40 percent said they had "no time to be nice."[5] A quarter said they were rude because their leaders were disrespectful. Another quarter reported that their companies lacked guidelines or training about how to treat people.

Technology is also straining workplace relationships. The average professional spends about six hours a day on e-mail, not counting time spent surfing the net, monitoring social media, or shopping online.[6] While electronic communication can bring us together in remarkable ways, it can lead to misunderstandings or gaps in communication, and it often liberates us to voice our frustrations, hurl insults, and take people down a notch from a safe distance. In addition, we spend so much time on computers that we often lose sight of how to connect with people face-to-face. We forget that others, like us, are human beings with needs and feelings.

Surveying these causes brings me to a crucial point, one of my biggest takeaways over the past couple of decades: *Incivility usually arises not from malice but from ignorance.* I started my research thinking that jerks out there were intentionally ruining workplaces; I now see that most bad behavior reflects a lack of self-awareness. We don't want to hurt others, but we do. A surgeon told me that until he'd received feedback, he had no idea that residents, nurses, and staff didn't like his harsh, directive style. Like the general manager at the start of this chapter, we're oblivious—and behaving in ways we'd never want to be treated.

Whether it's globalization, generational differences, workplace pressures, the fraying of workplace relationships, or technology, we seem to be more focused on ourselves and less on others. And to the extent that this is causing us to treat one another disrespectfully, it's costing us. In the next chapter, we'll take a closer look at the enormous toll incivility is taking on individuals, organizations, and society. As I think you'll agree, it's far from pretty.

KEY POINTS

- Incivility is in the eyes of the recipient. It's how people feel they are treated.

- Incivility is prevalent globally and has increased in the last two decades.

- We recognize the importance of connecting with others, yet we're choosing not to do so.

CHAPTER 2

Sidelined

I've learned that people will forget what you said, people will forget what you did, but people will never forget how you made them feel.

—Maya Angelou

Twenty-one years ago on Father's Day weekend, I walked into a warm, stuffy hospital room outside Cleveland, Ohio, to find my strong, vivacious dad lying helpless with electrodes strapped onto his bare chest. It turned out that Dad had suffered a heart attack scare. What caused it? No one knows, but since he was a generally healthy guy, I have a pretty good idea that it was job-related stress. For over a decade, my father had endured not one but two extremely uncivil bosses. It was ten years before he would talk about it, but when he did, he told me that his boss had made a habit of exploding in people's faces. He insulted employees, dismissed them, degraded their efforts, and blamed them for things over which they had no control. He was even uncivil to clients. During a visit to a client's store, my dad heard his boss tell the owner, "I see you're carrying on your father's tradition. This store looked like shit then, and it looks like shit in your hands."

For years, Dad put up with this, and it took a silent toll. Dad had never been the type to complain—at least not to us. He was more concerned with providing for our family. He had four kids and wanted to send us all to college, which wouldn't be easy. So he sucked it up. When times were tough, he explained how he was extremely grateful—to be born in America, where he had freedom, and also for his faith and his family. He felt very lucky to have met and married my mom.

Eventually, though, he just couldn't take it anymore. Worried about the effects his toxic boss was having on the organization, Dad mustered up the courage to talk to his corporate boss. He knew it was risky and told my mom, "If they don't fire him, I'm done." Within weeks, the bad boss was named District Manager of the Year. Days later, Dad was in the hospital.

When I entered the hospital room that day, Dad put on a brave face, even forcing a half smile, as if to convey to us that he was fine and we shouldn't worry. I could tell he was self-conscious and embarrassed— he didn't want us to see him like this. *I* didn't want to see him like this. Up until this point, he had seemed invincible. But incivility has a way of catching up with people. And with organizations too.

Stress: Deadlier than We Think

Modern science has a lot to tell us about the health impacts rudeness can have. Robert Sapolsky, author of *Why Zebras Don't Get Ulcers*, explains that when people experience intermittent stressors like incivility for too long or too often, they also experience significant health problems.[1] Incivility can deplete your immune system, causing cardiovascular disease, cancer, diabetes, and ulcers. For example, a 2012 study by the Harvard School of Public Health, which tracked women for ten years, concluded that stressful jobs were just as bad for women's health as smoking and obesity.[2]

Studies have found that "psychosocial" factors, such as work-related stress, are the most important variables in determining the length of a life.[3] While genes and associated risks matter, stress can be an even more significant factor. Arie Shirom at Tel Aviv University, and his colleagues, tracked eight hundred twenty adults who worked in various professions (from finance to manufacturing to healthcare) for twenty years. They interviewed these adults repeatedly about conditions at their jobs, the behavior of their managers, and the collegiality of their workmates—all while closely monitoring the participants' health. It wasn't the hours spent at work or other factors like workload, decision authority, or discretion that affected longevity. It was the positive support of coworkers. In fact, the presence of less-kind colleagues was associated with a much higher risk of dying.[4] Middle-aged employees with little or no "peer social support" in the workplace were 2.4 times more likely to die during the study.[5]

Research also shows that working in a group where incivility is present affects people's mental health, even after accounting for general stress and the incivility an individual personally experienced.[6] People tend to take the stress of incivility home with them, unleashing it on family members, who in turn carry the stress into their workplaces.[7] Conversely, another study found links between family incivility and stress and poor performance at work.[8]

A Hefty Toll

All of this costs organizations a *ton* of money, to put it mildly. The American Psychological Association estimates that workplace stress costs the US economy $500 billion a year.[9] A stunning 550 billion workdays are lost each year due to stress on the job, 60 to 80 percent of workplace accidents occur because of stress, and more than 80 percent of doctor visits are stress related. The National Institute for Occupational Safety and Health reports that workers who feel

16

stressed incur healthcare costs that are 46 percent higher than their less-stressed counterparts.[10] One of the greatest causes of stress—accounting for about half of it—is relationship difficulties at work.[11]

But higher healthcare costs and sick-day usage are just a few of the ways incivility hurts organizations. In a poll of eight hundred managers and employees across seventeen industries that I conducted with my colleague Christine Pearson, I learned that among workers who have been on the receiving end of incivility,

- 48 percent intentionally decreased their work effort,
- 47 percent intentionally decreased the time spent at work,
- 38 percent intentionally decreased the quality of their work,
- 80 percent lost work time worrying about the incident,
- 63 percent lost work time avoiding the offender,
- 66 percent said their performance declined,
- 78 percent said their commitment to the organization declined,
- 12 percent said they had left their job because of the uncivil treatment, and
- 25 percent admitted to taking their frustration out on customers.[12]

If organizations lose profits and employees thanks to incivility, much of this loss goes undetected. Employees who decide to quit based on an experience of bad behavior typically don't ever tell their employers why. Turnover costs add up quickly: four times an employee's annual salary in the case of high-level employees.[13]

And consider how much incivility drains managers' time. According to a study conducted by Accountemps and reported in *Fortune*, managers and executives of Fortune 1000 firms spend 13 percent of their time at work—the equivalent of seven weeks a year—mending employee relationships and dealing with the aftermath of incivility.[14] That's time *not* spent on core activities, like coming up with new strategies, getting close to customers, or mentoring employees. Costs soar even higher when companies bring in consultants or attorneys to help settle a situation.

Lost sales represent another area in which incivility can exact a large, hidden toll. Marketing professors Debbie MacInnis and Valerie Folkes and I have documented something most of us intuitively know: Customers don't like incivility.[15] In one of our experiments, we told participants that a marketing professor was helping a bank with an alumni credit card program.[16] Two members of our research team presented themselves as bank representatives, explaining that they were gathering opinions about possible new logos and alternative finance options. During the experiment, half the participants witnessed incivility between the two bank representatives (one reprimanded the other for not presenting credit card mock-ups in the right sequence). The other group witnessed no incivility.

We wondered whether consumers would change perceptions of an organization or its brand if they saw employees treating one another poorly. Boy, did they ever. The vast majority—almost 80 percent—of customers who hadn't seen the employees treat one another poorly said they would use the firm's products and services in the future. But only 20 percent of consumers who had witnessed the incivility said they would. And nearly two-thirds of participants who had witnessed the incivility said they would feel anxious dealing with *any* employee of this company. "I wouldn't go near that place again if they paid me!" one participant said.

I was surprised at how much customers disliked seeing rude behavior. I thought at least a few customers might have seen an employee do something wrong and, upon witnessing his or her colleague deliver a reprimand, think *Let her have it!* But we failed to find any incidents in which customers gave rude employees a pass. It didn't matter if the employee receiving the reprimand was incompetent or did something egregious (like parking in a handicapped spot). Witnesses simply did not approve of rudeness, regardless of the circumstances.

We theorized that maybe customers disliked incivility because it ruined their experience. When you go out for a nice meal at a restaurant, the last thing you want to see is someone being treated poorly, right? Actually, customers were just as upset about incivility that was taking place behind closed doors. Participants perceived incivility as morally wrong, and they didn't believe *any* person deserved to be treated badly.[17]

Plummeting Performance

As monumental as losses due to incivility are to companies, my colleagues and I suspected that incivility was exacting an even deeper toll because of the subtle ways in which it affected people's thinking skills. Amir Erez, a management professor at the University of Florida, and I decided to find out. We gathered together a group of college students and divided them into two groups. Members of one group experienced an instance of rudeness (a disparaging remark about college students generally). Members of the other group didn't (no remark was made about college students).

In each group, respondents were placed in situations in which they received identical treatment—the same person in the same context delivered the same basic form of neutral treatment or incivility. What varied were the *occasions* for the behavior. In one experiment, the experimenter was rude to participants for being late; in another, a complete stranger treated participants rudely; and in a third, we asked participants to simply think about how they would react to various types of uncivil encounters.

In each manipulated situation, we measured the participants' performance, creativity, and helping behaviors. To measure performance, we asked participants to complete anagram tasks (word scrambles). To measure creativity, we asked participants to brainstorm uses for common objects (like what to do with a brick) and we then rated the creativity and variety of their ideas. To measure helping behaviors, we provided opportunities for participants to help the experimenter (for instance, by picking up pencils that had been knocked over) and noted whether participants helped.

We found that even with one-time, low-intensity incidents, participants who had been treated uncivilly were not able to concentrate well—in effect, they were distracted from their work.[18] In the first part of the research, in which an experimenter belittled college students as a group (not participants personally), participants performed 33 percent worse on anagram tasks and came up with 39 percent fewer creative ideas during a brainstorming task we gave them. In the second experiment, in which on the way to the experiment participants encountered a stranger who behaved rudely (by admonishing them for bothering a busy professor), their performance was 61 percent worse on the anagram tasks, and they produced fewer than half as many ideas in the brainstorming task as those who had not been treated rudely. And those who merely witnessed incivility performed 20 percent worse on the anagrams and produced nearly 30 percent fewer ideas in the brainstorming task.[19]

As all of these experiments show, incivility robs you of your cognitive resources, hijacks your performance and creativity, and sidelines you from your work. Even if you want to perform at your best, you can't, because you're bothered and preoccupied by the rudeness. Chances are, you've experienced this firsthand. I know I have.

A powerful professor at my current university once cornered me at a holiday party and exclaimed, for all to hear, what a "f**ing stupid title" my book had. I said nothing in response, but I was mortified. Over the months that followed, I couldn't concentrate on my work; my mind often drifted to that interaction. Had I done something to provoke it? Would this professor's opinion affect my career? Should I have stuck up for myself? What should I do the next time I encountered this man? I spent too much time obsessing. It wasn't pleasant, and it certainly wasn't productive.

The Storm Inside Your Brain

Perhaps you're thinking I was too sensitive in that encounter with the professor, that I should have "gotten over it." But is it possible for people to just "get over" rudeness? My colleagues and I wondered that too, so we did an experiment.[20] First, we gave people combinations of words to use to make a sentence (we gave them five words to create a four-word sentence). Half the participants received words on their lists that could trigger or evoke rudeness—words like "aggressively," "bold," "bother," "obnoxious," "annoying," and "interrupt." A sample five-word combination of "they her bother see usually" could be unscrambled to read "they usually bother her." The other half of our participants received the same task, but the list of words contained no rude triggers, just neutral words like "send," "watches," and "rapidly." A five-word combination here would have been "they her send see usually," unscrambled as "they usually see her."

We wanted to know whether the mere presence of incivility in a person's mind disrupts attention and causes that person to "miss" critical information altogether, so we borrowed from the famous "invisible gorilla" manipulation devised by psychologists Daniel Simons and Christopher Chabris.[21] After participants completed the unscrambling exercise, we asked them to watch a video of a group of people playing basketball and to count the number of basketball passes made. Midway through the video, a person in a gorilla suit walked across the screen. Once the video concluded, participants wrote down how many passes they'd seen. Those who had seen the uncivil words during the unscrambling task were nearly *five times more likely* not to notice the gorilla. In other words, you can't "get over" incivility by sheer force of will. Rudeness affects your mind in ways you might not even be aware of, disrupting your ability to pay attention.

We also wondered if additional breakdowns occurred further along the cognitive process, disrupting executive control—the part of our cognitive systems responsible for planning, initiating activities, making decisions, and filtering out unnecessary information. We conducted another experiment, asking participants to remember a series of letters that flashed on a computer screen. Then we gave them math problems to complete and asked them to recall the letters—in order—that had been presented to them earlier. We found that those whom we had primed with uncivil words during the word scrambling task had a much more difficult time processing and recalling information. They recalled 17 percent less, performed 86 percent worse on the verbal tasks, and made 43 percent more mathematical errors than those who had not been primed with rude words.

Not spotting a gorilla or making mistakes on math is one thing, but being preoccupied with incivility in a hospital might be fatal. A doctor detailed to me how on one occasion a supervising doctor had belittled a medical team on duty. Soon after, the team accidentally administered the wrong treatment to a patient, ignoring vital information that had been *right there* on the chart. As a result, the patient died. A simple coincidence? Not quite. In a study of 4,500 doctors and nurses, 71 percent tied disruptive behavior (defined as "abusive personal conduct," including condescending, insulting, or rude behavior) to medical errors they knew of and 27 percent tied bad behavior to the deaths of their patients.[22] In another study of more than 800 physician executives, more than 70 percent said that disruptive behavior occurred in their hospitals at least once a month and almost everyone—99 percent—believed that bad behavior in their hospitals negatively affected their patients' care.[23]

Researchers have actually documented that incivility diminishes performance in medical settings. Twenty-four medical teams from four neonatal intensive care units in Israel were invited to a training workshop designed to improve quality of care. As part of the training, the teams needed to treat a premature infant whose condition suddenly deteriorated due to a serious intestinal illness (this was only a simulation; no infant's health was endangered). Staff had to identify and diagnose the condition and administer proper treatment, including CPR. Teams were told that an expert from the United States would be watching them remotely (via video) and would occasionally comment and advise them. That "expert" was a member of the research team. Half the teams received messages from a neutral expert, who spoke about the importance of training and practice using simulations but did not comment on their work quality. The other half received insulting messages about their performance and the "poor quality" of Israeli medical care.

Researchers filmed these simulations and had objective judges evaluate them. The teams exposed to rudeness displayed lower capabilities in *all* diagnostic and procedural performance metrics, markedly diminishing the infant's chances of survival. This was mainly because teams exposed to rudeness didn't share information as readily, and because they also stopped seeking help from their teammates.[24]

I frequently see this happening in my research: Lacking a sense of psychological safety, people shut down, often without realizing it. They are less likely to seek or accept feedback and also less likely to experiment, to discuss errors, and to speak up about potential or actual problems.[25] Even without an intimidator in the room with them, they work in a cloud of negativity and are unable to do their best.

Once incivility occurs, it's easy for negative thoughts to seep into people's heads and to stay there, translating into negative behavior. In experiments I've done, I've found that once people are exposed to rudeness, they are *three times less likely* to help others and their willingness to share drops by more than half.[26] It makes sense: When someone behaves poorly or offensively, bad feelings spread and behaviors escalate, sometimes even becoming aggressive. I see this happening at the companies with which I consult. At a large manufacturing company, an external consulting team was presenting their recommendations in a dismissive tone, setting off one of the company's executives. Verbal exchanges grew more heated and personal. "Let's take this outside!" an executive shouted. Like an episode from *The Office*, the room full of suits marched to the parking lot. Eventually, someone with a cooler head stepped in, preventing a fistfight. Can you imagine trying to focus after that incident?

Researchers have directly documented the negativity and outright aggression that incivility sparks in people's minds.

Here's an exercise for you: What word can you unscramble from these letters?

remdue = _ _ _ _ _ _

The correct answer is "demure." Did "murder" cross your mind? Our research has shown that if you witness incivility prior to this task, you're *eight times* more likely to provide that answer.[27]

Can Your Organization Afford These Losses?

People confronted with rudeness often behave like my dad did: They suck it up, thinking they're resilient and capable of rising above ridiculous circumstances. Yet, as we've seen, incivility has a way of pulling people off track and preventing them from doing their best. I've found this to be true in *every* study I've conducted. Even witnesses working around incivility take a hit. Incivility sucks something out of all of us. It takes us on an emotional roller-coaster ride.

It siphons cognitive resources. It even eats away at physical health. Ultimately, we become a fraction of ourselves. We don't show up to the same extent.

If you're experiencing incivility, don't brush it off. Seemingly minor words and deeds have an impact—not just on individuals but also on teams. It's time for us *all* to take it more seriously. Otherwise, the harm we cause or experience will likely build and perhaps, one day, become devastating.

KEY POINTS

- The human and business costs of incivility are much greater than you think.
- People experiencing incivility may struggle to get off the sidelines and back into the game.
- Customers punish organizations harshly for incivility, even if they don't witness it.
- Incivility impairs thinking. People miss information right in front of them.
- Those simply around incivility are more likely to have dysfunctional or aggressive thoughts, although they may be unaware of the connection.

CHAPTER **3**

Civility Buys Everything

Civility costs nothing, and buys everything.
                                        —M. W. Montagu

When I met Terri Kelly, CEO of the high-tech fabrics manufacturer W. L. Gore and Associates, I found her surprisingly low-key. Kelly was pulling her suitcase across the campus of the University of Southern California, where she had come to speak. She didn't have the usual handlers who accompany CEOs of large organizations (and Gore is large: ten thousand employees, with about $3 billion in annual revenue). Nobody was ushering her to the right place—no security, no personal assistant—and no fancy motorcade was in sight. When asking me for directions to the conference hall, she was humble, polite, and warm. She didn't seem interested in setting herself apart. She didn't flaunt her status. She seemed the very embodiment of civility.

I went to Kelly's presentation that day, and after learning about her unusual path to the CEO's office, I was even more impressed. Kelly first joined Gore in 1983 as a product specialist, eventually leading the unit before heading Gore's global fabrics division.

In 2005, Gore's then-CEO retired, and the board polled a wide cross-section of employees, asking them to choose a new leader. This is how things work at Gore: Associates become leaders based on their ability to gain their peers' respect. Anyone in the company could be nominated as the next CEO. Kelly's peers—the people with whom she'd worked for the past twenty-two years—chose her. This "surprised the heck out of me," Kelly explained, as there were other older and more obvious candidates vying for the job. But in the end, it was simple: Employees saw a respectful leader and team player they genuinely *wanted* to follow. Civility, you see, has a way of winning people over and garnering influence. The good guys, and gals, do win—more often than we think.

So far, we've focused on incivility—behavior that others perceive as rude or disrespectful. It's tempting to think that if you're not rude, then you're behaving in a civil fashion. In fact, you're only behaving in a neutral way; you haven't harmed anyone. Civility in the fullest sense requires something more: *positive gestures* of respect, dignity, courtesy, or kindness that lift people up. Think back to the introduction: You can either hold someone down through your actions or lift them up. Not holding someone down isn't the same as lifting them up. Not sidelining them isn't the same as encouraging their best self to shine forth.

Although civil behaviors entail treating others well, they must also reflect an underlying desire to show respect. It's not just treating someone well because you want something from them or because you're trying to serve your organization's interests. Civil behaviors are performed as a way of simply affirming norms of mutual respect and decency. I believe Kelly was warm, friendly, and kind for the same reason that all civil people are: We want to participate in a society that affords everyone a certain standard of attention, care, and nurturance.

In the workplace, civil behaviors can be extraordinarily small.

A colleague can smile and say hello to you in the hallway, an associate can ask an assistant to *please* do a task and *thank* her after she completes it. Leaders can behave civilly by engaging others in conversation rather than ordering them around, or by taking time to applaud subordinates when they do a good job. In an interview, Kelly explained that she self-consciously treats people in these ways: "The thing that's [different in our company] is how the leader conducts himself. The leader is there because they had the support from their peers, and they know that. They've got to earn that every day. They're not directing the organization, they're not telling. They're doing a lot of selling themself, in terms of why we should be doing this, and really getting the organization on board."[1]

Kelly further observes that leaders have to be more self-aware about "their flaws, their own behavior, and the impact they have on others." They should come across as "approachable and real" and should also live their company's culture, affirming through their actions the ideals the company holds dear.[2]

Not everyone thinks leaders should spend so much time caring about employee feelings and perceptions. Machiavelli famously said, "He who wishes to be obeyed must know how to command" and "It is much more secure to be feared than to be loved."[3] Many professionals I've met seem to agree, and they profess their skepticism about the returns of civility. They fear that people won't respect their authority if they take positive steps to treat people nicely; they believe they *have* to be tough, gruff, distant, domineering, and just plain rude to get ahead. In one survey of mine, nearly 40 percent of respondents were afraid that people would take advantage of them if they were nice at work. Nearly half thought that flexing their muscles was the best way to garner power.[4] Yet Kelly's story suggests that leaders can succeed *because* of civility and how they treat people, not in spite of it.[5]

Machiavelli Versus Terri Kelly

Jessica Kennedy of Vanderbilt University and I wondered whether being civil *cost* people status or power, or *secured* them those advantages. We began with an experiment that had participants read about one of two scenarios. We gave half of our participants a scenario about a talented doctor—we called him Dr. Jenner—who received complaints from his staff about his behavior. We described an instance in which Jenner exploded at one of his surgical assistants who had made an error during a rotator cuff surgery. His assistant apologized and explained how it had happened. The doctor responded by saying, "How can you be so incompetent? This guy has permanent nerve damage and it's your fault! Get out of my operating room!"

We told participants that Jenner had run-ins with anesthesiologists and gave nurses trouble whenever he had a bad day. But participants also learned that under Jenner's tutelage, residents had their pick of jobs afterward. They learned that although this doctor was unkind and rude to the staff, a few of the hospital's board members thought the world of him. This doctor "can absolutely turn on the charm," the scenario concluded. "Without a doubt, Jenner is irreplaceable in terms of intellectual and financial capital."

The other half of our participants read about a similar situation, except in this case, the doctor behaved in a civil fashion. This equally talented doctor never received complaints from staff about his behavior. When the surgical assistant apologized for making that very same mistake, the doctor responded by saying, "Generally, you are very competent. This guy has permanent nerve damage and we need to discuss whether it's our fault. For now, you can go home, but let's meet tomorrow." Participants learned that this doctor never clashed with anesthesiologists and treated nurses well even when he had a bad day. Like the doctor in the first scenario, this doctor churned out residents who had their choice of appointments at the end of their training. The doctor was kind and polite, and a few of the hospital's board members thought the world of him.

We compared the ratings of social status for participants who received the "respectful doctor" scenario with those who received the "rude doctor" scenario. We found a striking result: Participants rated the respectful doctor higher for social status and worthiness of respect and admiration. It wasn't a small difference either; the civil doctor was rated 36 percent higher for his social status. Machiavelli's contention that "it is much more secure to be feared than to be loved" seems *so* seventeenth century.[6]

In a second study, we rewrote the descriptions of the doctors' behavior to make it softer, less obvious. In the civility scenario, we noted that the doctor tended to smile, acknowledge everyone and their contributions, and humbly ask questions. The incivility scenario described the doctor as frowning, refusing to acknowledge anyone or their contributions, and aggressively asking questions. Although there was nothing overly dramatic, respondents still perceived the civil doctor as possessing a 78 percent higher social status. They saw him as 1.2 times more leader-like, 23 percent more competent, and—here's the kicker—16 percent more powerful.[7] Again, civility didn't tank someone's status or power in people's minds; it elevated it.

Movin' On Up

You might wonder whether civil people progress faster in their careers or if they get better results in their work. Yes, and yes![8]

Civil people usually have more opportunities for collaboration handed to them. Think about it: If you needed help from a colleague, would you call upon someone who was nice or someone who was more capable but a bit uncivil? Most people claim they would select the more capable one, arguing that ability is what counts. Yet their actions don't match up.

In a study of more than ten thousand work relationships, people chose colleagues for collaboration by asking the question "Do I enjoy working with her/him?" rather than the question "Does this person know what he/she is doing?"[9] If you treat people well, they're more excited to work with you. Over time, your reputation spreads, and still more people want to choose you over a possibly more talented but less civilized peer.[10]

I often see the power of civility at play when universities look to hire tenure-track professors. Rather than choose a superstar candidate with a reputation for being difficult or arrogant, departments will opt for a respectably productive but more civil colleague. As I've discovered, law firms and medical practices often make similar choices when recruiting senior attorneys and doctors; these are important, long-term hires, and nobody wants to saddle themselves and their organization with a rude colleague. When collaboration is crucial, civility counts even more. After a series of mergers, a consulting firm focused on retaining and promoting civil people who could interact well with others in multidisciplinary teams and communicate effectively across borders. If candidates didn't have strong interpersonal skills and an underlying mindset of kindness and respect, the consulting firm just didn't want to invest in them.

More generally, civility makes it far easier to build large and productive professional networks. In our modern age of social media, people believe they have to be active and engaged in order to have large networks. Maybe so, but civility should also be part of the mix. As our research has shown, people viewed as civil tend to occupy more important positions in networks. They serve as connectors of ideas, information, and people, and they are poised to cross boundaries more effectively in organizations.[11] More respectful people reap a windfall of networking and personal benefits, whereas those seen as uncivil get shut out of networks and all the benefits that come with them, such as information, advice, and career opportunities. In one study I did, participants were 1.2 times more likely to recommend a civil person for a job than an uncivil person.[12]

Civil behavior pays off in other ways too. If you're eager to move up the corporate ladder, people need to think of you as a leader. Studies I performed with Alexandra Gerbasi at the University of Surrey and Sebastian Schorch at the Universidad de los Andes showed that people tended to associate civility (defined in this study as treating someone respectfully, with dignity, politeness, or pleasantry) with being a leader. In a study we did at a biotechnology firm, those seen as civil were twice as likely to be viewed as leaders than those deemed uncivil, and they performed 13 percent better.[13]

Demonstrations of civility also help determine if people see someone as an *effective* leader. In a global study of over seventy-five thousand people, participants rated "caring," "cooperative," and "fair-minded" most highly among the characteristics of admired leaders.[14] A survey I performed of twenty thousand employees worldwide found that "demonstrating respect" was the most important leadership quality for garnering commitment and engagement.[15] As the authors of research who analyzed the findings from sixty-nine previous studies noted, "Leadership now, more than in the past, appears to incorporate more feminine relational qualities, such as sensitivity, warmth, and understanding."[16]

What ultimately helps people move up faster, of course, are the results they produce. And civility helps here too. Research confirms that small behaviors, such as thanking people, listening attentively, humbly asking questions, acknowledging others, sharing credit, or smiling, can give you a performance boost, while their converse—seemingly insignificant acts of *in*civility—can cost you. A good example of the latter: People tend to file malpractice suits because of poor medical care *and* how the patient feels about the doctor's behavior. One study compared doctors who get sued often with doctors who have never been sued. Those who had never been sued took more time to develop rapport with patients, talking to them an average of three minutes longer. There was no difference in the amount or quality of information given by the doctors; it was *how* the doctors talked to their patients that mattered. They educated patients more, laughed and used humor more, asked patients more questions, and humbly solicited patients' opinions.[17]

Nalini Ambady, former psychology professor at Stanford University, and her colleagues captured quick videos of conversations between surgeons and patients. They then had judges watch the tapes and rate the doctors on the basis of warmth, hostility, dominance, and anxiousness. Based on those ratings alone, researchers could correctly predict which surgeons got sued and which didn't.[18] Malcolm Gladwell summarizes this phenomenon eloquently in his book *Blink*: "Malpractice sounds like one of those infinitely complicated and multidimensional problems. But in the end it comes down to a matter of respect, and the simplest way that respect is communicated is through tone of voice, and the most corrosive tone of voice that a doctor can assume is a dominant tone."[19]

Ask yourself how *you* would fare if you were one of the surgeons in this study. Would you be among the professionals destined to get sued? If so, it really is time to improve your behavior.

Civility Cultivates Team and Organizational Wins

So far, I've been focusing on individuals, but research shows that civility enhances the performance of teams and organizations as well. A study of cross-functional product teams revealed that when leaders treated members of their team well, and fairly, the team members were more productive individually and as a team.[20] They also were more likely to go above and beyond their job requirements.

It all starts at the top. When leaders are civil, it increases performance and creativity;[21] allows for early mistake detection and the initiative to take actions;[22] and reduces emotional exhaustion.[23]

Consider the example of Costco founder Jim Sinegal. Regarding the retailer's customers and employees as more important than its shareholders, Sinegal made a point of visiting stores to simply say hello, a gesture he thought employees appreciated. He also made sure the company respected and rewarded its employees; Costco notably pays its workers an average hourly rate of $20.89, about 65 percent more than Walmart, the parent company of Costco's biggest competitor, Sam's Club.[24]

Over time, Costco's huge investment in its employees—including health benefits for part-time workers—has paid off. As Sinegal has said, "Imagine that you have 120,000 loyal ambassadors out there who are constantly saying good things about Costco. It has to be a significant advantage for you."[25] Costco's employees generate nearly twice the sales of Sam's Club employees. Moreover, they stay much longer with the company: Costco's turnover among employees who stay at least a year is very low by industry standards. Low turnover costs can save Costco several hundred million dollars a year. In addition, Costco has the lowest shrinkage (employee theft) in the industry.[26] Between 2003 and 2013, Costco's stock rose more than 200 percent, while Walmart's rose by only about 50 percent.[27]

Policies that demonstrate respect and care for people are good for business. But my experiments show that even brief, small gestures of civility help shape positive, value-adding behavior in teams and organizations. In one study, participants were 59 percent more willing to share information with people who behaved respectfully, 72 percent more likely to seek advice from them, and 57 percent more likely to seek information from them.[28]

Civility allows teams to function better in large part by helping employees feel safer, happier, and just plain *better.* Among employees in the study mentioned earlier of over twenty thousand employees, those who felt respected by their leader reported 56 percent better health and well-being, 89 percent greater enjoyment and satisfaction, 92 percent greater focus and prioritization, 26 percent more meaning and significance, and 55 percent more engagement.[29]

One of the most important ways civility enhances a team's performance is by increasing the amount of "psychological safety" people feel—the feeling that the team environment is a trusting, respectful, and safe place to take risks. One experiment of mine showed that psychological safety increased by 35 percent when people were offered a suggestion civilly as compared with uncivilly (i.e., in an interaction marked by inconsiderate interruption).[30] Other research has shown that psychological safety also improves general team performance. Studying more than 180 of its active teams, Google found that *who* was on a team mattered less than *how* team members interacted, structured their work, and viewed their contributions. Employees on teams with more psychological safety were more likely to make use of their teammates' ideas and less likely to leave Google. They generated more revenue for the company and were rated as "effective" twice as often by executives.[31]

It's All About the *How*

"Performance is not just what you do," Microsoft's general manager of talent and organization capability Vicki Lostetter told me, "but *how* you do it. That's critical." The many studies described in this chapter have borne that out. To make the greatest impact in your business and to get the most out of your career, choose the path of respectfulness over rudeness. It paid off for Arthur Demoulas, CEO of the New England grocery chain Market Basket. Demoulas went out of his way to learn many of his twenty-five thousand employees' names and to greet them warmly when he visited.[32] He paid workers well over the minimum wage and maintained a profit-sharing plan even during the financial downturn.[33] When he was ousted, thousands of employees—and customers—took to the streets to show support for him. The rallies helped pave the way for Demoulas to buy out his cousin, who ran the board, and regain control over the company.[34] Demoulas explained, "If everyone in the workplace is equal and treated with dignity, they work with a little extra passion, a little extra dedication."[35]

Civility is smart. It's savvy. It's human. By being civil, you get to be a nice person *and* you get ahead. What could be better than that? People are more likely to support you and work harder for you in turn.

You might object that some leaders seem to succeed even though they behave uncivilly. I would counter that those people have succeeded *despite* their incivility. Studies have shown that the number one characteristic associated with an executive's failure is an insensitive, abrasive, or bullying style, while number three is aloofness or arrogance.[36] Sure, power can force compliance, but insensitivity or disrespect can sabotage support in crucial situations. Employees may fail to share important information or withhold efforts or resources; payback may come immediately or when uncivil leaders least expect it. And no one can say if it's intentional or unconscious.

Whether you're a CEO, a team leader, or a person from any walk of life trying to make a difference, you're going to be judged for the little moments, so please make the most of them. In every interaction, you have a choice. Do you want to lift people up or hold them down? Who do *you* want to be?

Be brave. Try civility on. My bet is that others will like it. And so will you.

Civility Buys Everything

- Individuals feel valued and powerful when respected. Civility lifts people, and teams and businesses along with them.

- Small, civil gestures make a difference.

- Rude people succeed despite their incivility, not because of it.

CHAPTER 4

The Incivility Bug

When once the forms of civility are violated, there remains little hope of return to kindness or decency.

—Samuel Johnson

Remember the nightmare job I had launching a sports academy at a global athletic brand? Back in those days, the academy had a well-equipped gym (among other facilities) where professional athletes and academy members would work out. I used to show up early to exercise at the gym with friends and colleagues, including coaches, trainers, and management staff. Some days, our uncivil leader showed up, and he would immediately blast the fitness director for piping fast-paced workout music over the loudspeaker system: Why wasn't the leader's favorite music playing?! (By the way, the leader's favorite music was Barry White—not exactly the kind of music that peps you up while you run or pump iron.)

The leader's verbal lashing of the director seemed to go on forever. It took place in front of everybody, including the director's wife, who also worked out there. The director raced back to the office and fumbled with the music, trying to correct the situation as quickly as he could. In a matter of moments, Barry White's velvety voice echoed throughout the building.

That didn't assuage the leader, though. He was still upset, so he continued to rant and rave at the director. It was awkward for everyone. When the leader finally left, we all breathed a sigh of relief. Yet none of us had our usual energy. Our day had soured, and it wasn't even 6:30 a.m.

I often brought athletes to the fitness center for specialized workout sessions. On the days when the leader was uncivil, I noticed that the coaches and trainers who worked with these athletes weren't at their best. They were unfocused, unmotivated, and in foul moods, even though the leader's tirade hadn't been directed at them. This, in turn, colored the athletes' experience. Their workouts weren't what they could be, and *their* moods soured. Sometimes they went off on the managers who shadowed them or they were nasty to the cafeteria staff. The people who were eating lunch with the grumpy athletes picked up on the unpleasant vibe, and *their* moods also began to darken.

Many people think of rudeness as a self-contained experience, limited to one person or interaction. In truth, incivility is a virus that spreads, making the lives of everyone exposed to it more difficult. In a typical corporate headquarters, incivility might start in one office, and before you know it, it's down the hall, up three floors, and in the break room, infecting someone who may have contact with clients and customers. Left unchecked, incivility can drag down an entire organization, making everyone less kind, less patient, less energetic, less fun—simply *less*.

The Making of an Emotional "Plague"

We each have a much bigger effect on one another's emotions than we might think—for better and for worse. In their book *Connected*, Nicholas Christakis and James Fowler show how happiness spreads not only among pairs of people but also between a person and his friends, his friends' friends, and their friends.[1] If a friend of a friend of a friend of yours becomes happier, this can positively affect you. Research with a professional male cricket team shows that a player's happiness influences the happiness of his teammates; when teammates are happier, overall team performance improves.[2] Happiness in this context doesn't depend on deep, personal connections; frequent, superficial, face-to-face interactions can also powerfully influence happiness.

Civility and incivility spread the same way. A seemingly small act of kindness or rudeness ripples across communities,[3] affecting people in our network with whom we may or may not interact directly.

On a non-conscious level, people become aware of the concept of rudeness when they're around it in any form, even when they aren't the target of it directly.[4] A node in the brain is activated, and this activation rapidly spreads across the neural network to nearby nodes.[5] In practical terms, a rude e-mail you read might activate nodes in your brain associated with memories of other encounters in which you experienced or witnessed rudeness. In your mind, the activated concepts—in this case, rudeness and incivility—become more accessible; they come to mind and can shape your judgments and decision making.

An experiment conducted by Elizabeth Loftus and John Palmer during the 1970s illustrates why some people may be more sensitive to rudeness than others. Loftus and Palmer showed one group of participants a series of videos depicting car accidents and then asked participants how fast the cars were going when they hit each other. They then asked the other set of participants a similarly worded question but replaced the word "hit" with words of a harder tone, such as "smashed," or "collided." Perhaps not surprisingly, the participants whose questions contained verbs associated with high speed judged the speeds as faster than those whose questions contained verbs associated with lower speeds. Loftus and Palmer hypothesized that the wording made concepts associated with high speeds more accessible in people's minds, influencing the way they judged the situation.[6]

In an office setting, if someone recently experienced rudeness, they will likely perceive greater rudeness while working on subsequent projects than a teammate who didn't experience rudeness recently. They are tuned in to incivility—not because they are "sensitive people" but because past experiences have primed them to pick up on incivility more acutely.

Sneaking into Our Subconscious

In general, our minds are very sensitive; it doesn't take much for incivility to affect us—even a single word thrown our way can make a big difference in how we behave. In one study, Charles Carver of the University of Miami and his colleagues told participants that they were taking part in a "learning experiment" in which they would be "teaching" another participant (actually a member of the research team) by administering rewards for correct answers and punishments for incorrect answers. To dole out punishments, they would deliver an electric shock at a length of their choosing. (Obviously these were not real electric shocks. No researchers were harmed in the making of this experiment!)

Just before researchers finished giving out the instructions, another experimenter entered the room and explained that she was almost finished with her master's thesis project, but some of her participants had failed to show up. She asked participants if they would complete a form for her study. All the participants agreed and completed the form. Little did they know that the researchers had manipulated the document: Some of the forms contained hostile words (such as "rude" or "aggravating"), while others didn't contain hostile words. Participants then engaged in the alleged "learning experiment" in which they gave "shocks" to a "learner."

What do you think happened? The participants researchers had primed with hostile words were more likely to give much longer shocks to the learner.[7] When you're exposed to hostility or aggression, you behave differently. Incivility sneaks into your subconscious. It's easy to see how plagues of incivility can take shape and spread.

Now, most of us don't have the opportunity to shock other people during the course of our workdays. We do, however, have many opportunities to interrupt other people as they're speaking. In my surveys, interrupting is the rude behavior most often attributed to bosses.[8] Researchers in another study wondered if people exposed to words related to rudeness (e.g., "bother," "disturb," "annoyingly," "interrupt," "obnoxious") would more often interrupt someone during a lengthy conversation than someone exposed to words related to politeness (e.g., "courteous," "polite," "considerate," "appreciate," "graciously"). The results were stunning: While 67 percent of participants exposed to rude words interrupted the conversation—some more aggressively than others—only 16 percent of participants exposed to polite words chose to interrupt.[9]

Just because someone exposes you to rudeness doesn't mean you're doomed to be uncivil to others, though. When you follow a rude experience—like the one at the gym—with a polite one, the polite one "overwrites" the rude one, loosening the hold it has on your mind. So next time you witness or are a victim of rudeness, "reprogram" your mind by purposefully exposing yourself to something more positive. At the sports academy, I'd talk to my friendly civil colleague for a few minutes or I'd read an e-mail or text that evoked a spirit of kindness. Such experiences don't merely serve as a kind of balm; they inoculate you against the "virus" of incivility. (Please see chapter 14 for how to handle uncivil situations.)

Bubbles

I recently spoke with the CEO of a company who wasn't sure what to do about a high-level executive who treated people horribly. On the one hand, his employees were greatly disturbed by the executive's conduct, and the CEO feared things would only get worse if the executive stayed. On the other hand, the executive had made a fortune for the company, he was well known in a small industry, and the company would not have been nearly what it was without his efforts and talent. The executive was also a longtime friend of the CEO and had helped him greatly over the course of his career. After weighing his options, the CEO decided to put him on leave. The CEO wanted his organization to recover and thrive, and the only way to do that was to extricate the virus of incivility from the working environment.

When the executive returned, the CEO removed him from all interactions with employees, placing him, in effect, in a self-contained bubble. The CEO then let the employees of his organization know that they didn't need to worry anymore; while the executive would have a formal relationship with the company, he wouldn't be within harm's reach.

I've seen companies deploy this "bubble" strategy several times, and I can tell you it usually works. A Fortune 500 high-tech firm I worked with had acquired a much smaller firm to help them develop a product. This little firm's founders behaved poorly, dragging people within the larger organization down. Initially, the larger organization cut the smaller firm loose, but it turned out they needed the smaller firm's technology. So they acquired the smaller firm again, but this time they placed the larger organization's offices off-limits. They had experienced the viral effects of incivility, and they weren't willing to make themselves vulnerable again.

Brain Burn

Don't think of the bubble strategy as the perfect fix for incivility, though. While an incivility bug may be knocked into submission, it also may lie dormant within us, tattooed on our brains. As Dr. Edward Hallowell notes, bad memories can stick around for years—what Hallowell calls "brain burn."[10] When someone experiences difficult or unpleasant rudeness, a rush of emotions can cause physiological responses (e.g., increased heart rate, erratic breathing) and a flooding of intense emotions. Anger, fear, and sorrow may arise simultaneously, overwhelming the target or witness of incivility and leaving a scar that is both psychological and physical. High levels of adrenaline pump through the body in these situations, burning a hole in the brain, creating a permanent "tattoo." Once this happens, the overwhelming emotions are never forgotten; the simple sight of the offender or the place where the incident occurred may rekindle these feelings.

Recently, when I returned to the gym where I used to work, I vividly recalled all the unpleasant mornings I had suffered there. Even though my colleagues and I had had lots of fun together—great workouts, Thanksgiving pick-up football games, memorable celebrations of birthdays and other events—my mind still drifted to those episodes of rudeness. And I hadn't even been the target! Yet somehow, over twenty years later, I could still tell you exactly what had happened.

Scientists have long known that the amygdala, a small, almond-shaped sector in the brain, triggers emotional responses.[11] If an employee's cubicle is near her boss's office and she frequently overhears her boss treating others badly, that pattern can hijack her amygdala, burning a negative emotion into her brain. Every time this employee looks at her boss's door, she might experience negative emotions.

As a result, it may not take much for the incivility bug to rear its ugly head, even after an offender has been placed inside a bubble.

Relatively minor incidents—when people thoughtlessly put down others, for instance, or question their capabilities publicly—leave an imprint, whittling away at them, their performance, and their well-being. As a mathematical model developed by Yale psychologists Adam Bear and David Rand showed, people who are typically surrounded by jerks learn intuitively to be selfish and also not to deliberate over their actions. They wind up acting selfishly even when cooperating would pay off, precisely because they don't stop to think.[12] Our environment rubs off on us, and if our environment is toxic, we can expect to stay somewhat sick and to pass it on to others.

To beat the bug, we need to take steps to detoxify ourselves (a subject I'll cover more fully in chapter 14).

Primed for Politeness

If incivility can spread rapidly, its effects lingering long after the initial instance of rudeness, then civility can too. In a study of a biotech firm, my colleagues and I documented that when employees are civil in small ways (e.g., being attentive, smiling, not interrupting), their behavior is likely to be reciprocated and spread between colleagues.[13] But I don't need a formal study to prove this; I see it happening all the time in my daily life.

At Reagan Airport in Washington, DC, where I often go when I travel, there's an Alaska Airlines employee who just radiates positivity and delights everyone around her. On some occasions, even when there's frigid weather outside and passengers are impatient and demanding, this woman somehow still has it all under control. She handles everyone respectfully, with a smile. Not only do I feel better just watching her, but I also see people's expressions change after a brief encounter with her. The Alaska Airlines crews and passengers head off to their destinations happier and primed for more politeness.

Passengers and crew are just a little nicer to one another. They help one another more readily. They are more patient with one another. And after their flights, they disembark their planes with less edge.

Louisiana's Ochsner Health System, a large healthcare organization, appreciated the viral effects of civility so much they created a formal policy designed to harness it. Under Ochsner's 10/5 Way, you make eye contact and smile if you're within ten feet of someone, and you say hello if you're within five feet.[14] When this policy came into effect, the organization saw civility spread. Patient satisfaction scores rose, as did patient referrals.

As we've seen, incivility is not typically an isolated incident. It's highly infective and invasive, a pathogen that can quickly and silently sicken a team, department, and organization as well as customers and other external stakeholders. Most people may not realize just how susceptible they are and the extent to which they are carriers of it. Fortunately, civility's power to spread is just as great. It's up to us to gird ourselves against rudeness, to fight back hard when it's expressed, and to do everything we can to spread kindness and joy to those around us. Each one of us, through even the smallest of actions, has the capacity to create an atmosphere that's warm, affirming, and energizing. We can do it today—right now. What's stopping you?

KEY POINTS

- The effects of your words and deeds ripple far beyond the people working directly with you. If you're uncivil to someone, expect that he or she will pass it on.

- Placing offenders in a "bubble" can contain incivility, although not necessarily eradicate it.

- When you're civil, you contribute to a cycle that fosters greater civility across all your networks.

II

Civility Checkup: How You Are Doing and How You Can Improve

Part 2 of this book will help you cultivate civility in your own behavior. All these behavior shifts will help you become your best, most effective self.

CHAPTER 5

Are You Civil?

Everyone thinks of changing the world, but no one thinks of changing himself.

—Leo Tolstoy

So far, we've covered what incivility is, the costs it levies on individuals and organizations, and how it spreads rapidly. We've also highlighted some potential wins you gain by being civil.

Now it's time to get real: *Are you civil?*

This chapter gives you the tools and advice you need to take an honest look at yourself and your behavior. My goal here isn't to determine whether you're the "jerk in the office." Rather, I want to help you gain more self-awareness so you can make necessary adjustments and behave more intentionally.

Regardless of how well behaved we think we are, we *all* can become kinder and more considerate. If you look at the most successful people in any field, you almost always find they are constantly working to improve their game. Look more closely at how you treat other people, and face up to whatever uncomfortable truths might emerge. As the author Bryant McGill has written, "Change will never happen when people lack the ability and courage to see themselves for who they are."[1]

As a great deal of research has shown, all of us are inclined to see ourselves in a more favorable light; leadership coach and author Marshall Goldsmith calls this the "highlight reel of our successes."[2] My favorite example of such "self-serving bias" comes from a study by Francesca Gino at Harvard Business School, in which many participants rated their chances of getting into heaven more likely than those of Mother Teresa.[3]

Take the Incivility Test

Look closely and systematically at how you treat others. The following quiz I created (found at http://cycletocivility.com/) is designed to help you identify areas of high and low civility and to offer specific, actionable recommendations to make you more civil in the workplace.[4] I previously presented this quiz to an international law firm and have used it in courses for executives and MBA students.[5] I even included it in a blog post I wrote for Google's website re:Work, which garnered some great data and interesting results.[6] When I published a portion of the quiz in the *New York Times*,[7] I was inundated with e-mails and calls, many from consulting firms around the world who wanted to use it to learn how client firms stacked up. People who've taken this quiz have often reported gaining revelations into their behaviors. For example, the quiz made one friend realize that he tended to use e-mail even when the information really should have been delivered face-to-face. Others fessed up to not listening well because they were constantly checking their e-mail during meetings.

In taking this quiz, be honest with yourself. Assume that you're biased, inclined to see your behavior as more positive than it really is. Use this quiz proactively to catch behaviors you might not have thought about and to prevent yourself from developing some pretty bad habits. Use it as well to highlight some of the positive things you often do but might waffle on, depending on the circumstances. When answering the questions, be sure to think about specific people you work with, especially those you don't particularly care for. Think about habits you've developed, particularly those you wish you hadn't. Try to remember feedback that close friends and colleagues may have given you, especially the type that is hard to swallow. And, once again, *be honest*.

Do you ever do any of these?

	never	almost never	sometimes	quite a lot	almost always
Neglect to say please and thank you	☐	☐	☐	☐	☐
Use e-mail when face-to-face communication is needed	☐	☐	☐	☐	☐
Take too much credit for collaborative work	☐	☐	☐	☐	☐
E-mail or text during meetings	☐	☐	☐	☐	☐
Keep people waiting needlessly	☐	☐	☐	☐	☐
Talk down to others	☐	☐	☐	☐	☐
Delay access to information or resources	☐	☐	☐	☐	☐
Use jargon even when it excludes others	☐	☐	☐	☐	☐
Pass the blame when you've contributed to a mistake	☐	☐	☐	☐	☐
Spread rumors	☐	☐	☐	☐	☐
Belittle others nonverbally (e.g., roll your eyes, smirk)	☐	☐	☐	☐	☐

MASTERING CIVILITY

Retreat into your e-gadgets	☐	☐	☐	☐	☐
Shut someone out of a network or team	☐	☐	☐	☐	☐
Take advantage of others	☐	☐	☐	☐	☐
Pay little attention or show little interest in others' opinions	☐	☐	☐	☐	☐
Don't listen	☐	☐	☐	☐	☐
Set others up for failure	☐	☐	☐	☐	☐
Ignore invitations	☐	☐	☐	☐	☐
Show up late or leave a meeting early with no explanation	☐	☐	☐	☐	☐
Insult others	☐	☐	☐	☐	☐
Fail to acknowledge others and their efforts	☐	☐	☐	☐	☐
Belittle others and their efforts	☐	☐	☐	☐	☐
Make demeaning or derogatory remarks to someone	☐	☐	☐	☐	☐
Take others' contributions for granted	☐	☐	☐	☐	☐
Grab easy tasks while leaving difficult ones for others	☐	☐	☐	☐	☐
Forget to include others	☐	☐	☐	☐	☐

Are You Civil?

Speak unkindly of others	☐	☐	☐	☐	☐
Write uncivil or rude e-mails	☐	☐	☐	☐	☐
Behave disrespectfully when disagreeing with others	☐	☐	☐	☐	☐
Interrupt others	☐	☐	☐	☐	☐
Avoid looking out for others	☐	☐	☐	☐	☐
Judge people who are different from you	☐	☐	☐	☐	☐

So how did you do? What are you doing and saying that spreads incivility? What are you missing? Are you lifting or squashing others? Again, don't get down on yourself if you do many of these. Some of us have an advantage: We are genetically predisposed to be nice due to hormone levels.[8] But in the end, we're all human. The point is to improve your behaviors unearthed by this quiz.

Think carefully about cause and effect. What leads you to be less than civil? Do certain people push you over the edge? Do you think you're gaining something by being uncivil? Do you find yourself less capable of managing your feelings and actions at certain times of the day? Do certain places cause the beast to rise within you? And what are your triggers? Unfair treatment? Disrespect? Arrogance? Competition? Stress? What forces you to be less than your best self? Once you understand better when, where, and how you're inclined to behave rudely, and the forms such rudeness takes, you can be more mindful of when you're in the danger zone, or rapidly approaching it.

I often take this test myself, and when I do, I'm not always happy with what I learn. Yet I find it helpful to see my bad habits more clearly, which can prevent future incivilities. In the moment just before I'm about to do something I probably won't be proud of, a thought might bounce to the forefront of my mind: *Who do I want to be?* Once the answer takes shape in my mind's eye, how I should behave becomes a lot clearer.

If I'm going to experience a challenging situation, or if I know I'll need to handle something difficult with tact, I try to schedule it when I'll be at my best (not late afternoon or beyond!). And if I know I'll be in a tough environment or with people who trigger me, I make a special effort to coach myself through it. I tell myself to bite my tongue if I'm itching to say something I might regret. I focus on the phrase that helps me the most: *Who do I want to be?* I remind myself that I don't want to leave a bad impression or feel regrets. I know what this environment or people do to me, and I fight my inner tendencies. Over time, I will spot improvements in my behavior.

Hone In on Your Blind Spots

This quiz is a great start, but I'd encourage you to seek additional feedback from colleagues, friends, and family, since there still may be parts of your behavior you've missed.[9] Most of us miss elements of how we behave, both large and small. In fact, in business, political opinion polling, and speed dating, behavior in our blind spots accounts for approximately 40 percent of variation in success.[10] Tone of voice is a good example. One study suggests that the tone others use with us accounts for 38 percent of what we process from a conversation.[11] Accurately evaluating our own tone of voice is really tough—and for good reason. By the time we reach four months old, our superior temporal sulcus (STS) is sorting all auditory information, and by the ripe age of seven months, we use our STS to pick up the emotional content of a person's tone. Yet when we speak, the STS turns off![12] Yes, we can hear our own voice, but not the same way everyone else hears it.

We have plenty of other blind spots too, such as our facial expressions. We may feel ourselves smile, but we often don't sense other facial movements, such as our eyebrows shooting up in shock, fear, or disgust.[13] As you feel judgment racing in, are you really able to hide it?

Other factors can magnify the impact our blind spots have. When we fail at something, for instance, we might attribute it to circumstantial factors, while others tend to attribute it to our character.[14] If you're late, you may brush it off by pointing to traffic or a phone call you just had to take. The person waiting for you will likely be less forgiving, especially if lateness is your pattern. They'll chalk it up to you and your choices.

Another factor is the gap that exists between the intent and impact of our actions. You gave a colleague some critical (developmental) feedback; she felt like you belittled her—in front of the whole team. As Douglas Stone and Sheila Heen point out in their book *Thanks for the Feedback*, we judge ourselves by our intentions, while others judge us by the effects of our actions.[15] We don't get as much credit as we'd like for trying. If we fare poorly in how we execute something—such as delivering feedback poorly—then others count it against us. Any blind spots we might have seem to loom ever larger to others.

To make matters worse, we often don't realize the general impact we have on others. During my first year at a new university, a well-meaning colleague offered me some career advice, suggesting that I had been playing on the "junior varsity team," since I was teaching undergraduates. That comment really cut me; she was implying that I wasn't good enough to play on the "varsity team" with the bigwigs. I vividly recall feeling like a shrunken, defensive, powerless shadow of myself while listening to her. As a former athlete, I was especially sensitive to this comment, and I was defensive because I had taught MBAs for many years elsewhere. In addition, this woman had loomed over me as she spoke, looking down at me with a stern, judgmental expression on her face. I don't think she was out to get me. She meant to help, but she clearly lacked awareness of her blind spots. As a result, she came off as much harsher than she might have intended.

How deeply do you understand your most minute social behaviors? To gain the self-awareness you need, you must solicit others' help. Ask others to serve as an honest mirror for you, using the following seven simple strategies:

Strategy #1: Ask for Focused Feedback on Your Best and Worst Behaviors

Want to feel good and reinforce what you're doing well? Try a technique developed by Laura Roberts of Antioch University and her colleagues:[16] Collect feedback from about ten to fifteen people—including coworkers, friends, and family—about your most respectful self. Ask for positive examples of your best behavior. How, specifically, have others seen you treat people well? What was the context, what happened, and what did you do to make others feel valued? How did you lift others up?

After compiling the feedback, look closely for recurring commonalities. You might use Wordle.net—an online tool that generates a colorful word-based picture—to identify the qualities that create your best and most civil self. When, where, how, and with whom are you at your best? Organize the commonalities into themes and record your thoughts on them into a chart similar to the following:

Are You Civil?

Theme	Example(s)	My thoughts
You treat others as equals, as part of the team.	"I didn't feel like you were above me. You saw me as your partner. Because of that, I felt more willing to speak up and share ideas for how to improve things."	I should continue to try to do things to make people feel valued. I want to communicate that they matter and that I want to hear from them. Be mindful of little things, like where I sit at the table. Ask people, especially those with less status, "What do you think?"
You are warm, friendly, and thoughtful; people know you care.	"You wrote me a beautiful, handwritten thank-you note. I never get those anymore!" "You baked my favorite cookies for my birthday and wrote me a really thoughtful card." "Even though you were really busy and traveling, you took the time to call me and ask about my medical test. It wasn't a major test, but I was really nervous about it. It meant a lot that you remembered and called that day."	Do the little things! They matter to people. Take the time. Write the note. Make the call. Ask how they're doing (and genuinely mean it). Show up for people when they need it.

Don't stop there. Be sure to also gather candid feedback from others on areas for improvement (please see the Actions and Impact for Your Group and Organization section). Identify a couple of trusted colleagues who have your best interests in mind, and ask them for their impressions on how you treat other people. What do you do well? What could you do better? Listen carefully, and identify at least one change you want to make. Then have a separate set of conversations in which you gather specific information on how best to make that improvement. This part of the "feed forward" process, as author Marshall Goldsmith has noted, involves five steps:

1. Describe your goal clearly.
2. Ask for suggestions.
3. Listen carefully.
4. Thank the person; don't make excuses or get defensive.
5. Repeat this process with additional people.[17]

If you use this approach, you'll wind up with concrete suggestions from a number of people invested in your success. You'll be in a great position to hit the ground running. Be sure to check in periodically with these people, because they can help you gauge your improvement over time.

Strategy #2: Work with a Coach

Coaches can uncover your potential weaknesses by independently surveying and interviewing your colleagues and by shadowing you at meetings and events. A great coach can detect subtleties in your behavior of which you might not be aware, and can identify underlying assumptions, experiences, and personal qualities that make you prone to uncivil behavior.[18] A talented coach can also help you figure out practical behavioral improvements and hold you to them.

An entertainment firm in Hollywood brought in a coach to work with a young female attorney who was fighting with her lead attorney. She had brashly told him that he "wasn't doing things right" and that "this wasn't how it was done", at the previous firm where she'd worked. In addition, she would come in late to work and lash out at others when frustrated. The coach learned very quickly that this young woman was unhappy for legitimate reasons. Although she had been hired as an associate, the work she was being assigned was that of a paralegal. She also hadn't been given the kind of control over her work hours that associates at the firm typically enjoyed. The coach pinpointed this woman's triggers and spoke candidly about what was best for her. The woman recognized that she didn't like the person she was becoming and decided to find a firm better suited to her goals and desires. Everybody won.

Strategy #3: Conduct a Team Tune-Up: Use Colleagues or Friends as Coaches

Not everyone has access to coaches. Who else can you enlist to help you become more effective? I have MBAs and executives coach one another. This has been a very effective and cost-efficient way to improve civility and social intelligence.

Making progress on civility doesn't have to be a solitary endeavor; you can and should do it alongside other members of your team. While you're working to improve your own behavior, encourage your team members to do the same. Have an open discussion with your team about what you and your teammates do or say that conveys respect. How or when are you and your teammates less than civil to each other? What could you do or say better? Discuss what the team will gain by being more respectful of one another. As the entire team develops new norms, hold one another accountable for them.

You might try taking the quiz I presented at the beginning of this chapter with your colleagues. When I use the quiz with groups, the conversation often begins before people have even put down their pencils. "Do I ever talk down to others?" someone will say. "Do you ever!" a colleague will reply. Colleagues will spontaneously coach one another and offer candid feedback: "Hey, man, share the credit more often!" or "You'd be more effective if you were more direct." Or "Try to be on time more." Such open communication is the first step toward enhanced team performance.

Use the "Who's in Your Group?" exercise (found in the Actions and Impact for Your Group and Organization section) to indicate who in the group demonstrates particular positive or negative behaviors. I also have teammates complete an index card for each member, providing specific suggestions for how each person might behave more effectively. On one side of the card, participants provide information on strengths: What should the person keep doing to be his or her best, most civil self? On the other side of the card, they identify three things the teammate should work on to become more influential: What subtle nonverbals or habits might be limiting their potential? What might the person adjust to enhance his or her civility?

You might be surprised by how valuable and insightful this feedback is. Give it a shot!

Strategy #4: Get 360 Feedback

Identify one behavior you'd like to change. This could have come from the civility test or from others' feedback, including performance reviews. Then solicit feedback from your teammates, direct reports, and managers—"360 feedback"—about how you might change. Ask colleagues to help you by holding you accountable. In his book *What Got You Here Won't Get You There*, Marshall Goldsmith shares how he learned from his own 360-degree evaluation that he had a habit of making destructive comments about his employees behind their backs.[19] He felt terrible and vowed to his staff that he would change. He promised ten dollars to anyone who caught him making these uncivil comments. Although Goldsmith was afraid employees might not speak up, he soon found that some even goaded him into making such comments in order to get the reward. By noon on the first day, he was out fifty dollars. His method worked; each day he improved. The second day, he racked up only thirty dollars in penalties, followed by ten dollars the day after that. It didn't take him very long to break his rude habit entirely.

Your 360 feedback can take many forms, and I encourage you to make it fun. At a university where I worked, faculty established "insider signals" for bad behavior—hand signs for faculty members to coach one another about their offensive behavior during meetings. The "yellow card" sign (fist raised to the side of the head) meant that a speaker's tone or intensity was getting abrasive. The "red card" sign (two fingers held up, followed by the classic heave of the thumb) meant that it was time for the speaker to stop. Professors learned to restrain themselves and keep quiet at the red card signal. It was a fun and effective technique that kept us all mindful of incivility, in others and in ourselves.[20]

Feedback from colleagues shouldn't be just critical. Ask your team to let you know when they see small improvements. One executive enlisted her team to help her change a specific behavior: her tendency to constantly interrupt people in meetings and take over their ideas. Working with a coach, the executive developed a technique for avoiding this pattern: She would tap her toe instead of interrupting. She informed her team that she was working on this behavior, and after a couple of days of meetings, she checked in with them about her progress. The team was impressed that she was making an effort and that she had shown some vulnerability. They relished the opportunity to help her improve, and they appreciated the benefits. A norm of open dialogue was established, with team members counting on one another to help facilitate their growth.

Strategy #5: Teach Yourself How to Read Emotions

If you struggle to read or to provide warm body language and facial expressions, there are many things you can do on your own to up your game. Based on many years of research, here is my go-to list of tips:

• Observe others closely as you go about your day, especially people who seem to be great at civility. Paul Ekman, professor emeritus at the University of California, San Francisco, has found that we can improve our ability to identify people's emotions simply by studying facial expressions.[21]

• Use emotional intelligence quizzes and tools to test how well you're able to read others and their emotions. You might also test how reactive you are to others. (See the Recommended Resources section.)

• Play games with others. Research in neuroscience shows that when we compete against someone, our brain creates a "mental model" of the other person's emotions and intentions.[22] This allows us to bolster our awareness of their emotional state.

• Explore and develop your imagination. Research shows that people who read fiction are more attuned to others' emotions and intentions.[23]

• Watch one of your favorite television shows or movies and focus on the interactions of specific characters. Describe the feelings communicated and try to imagine what has triggered those emotions. Pay particular attention to facial gestures and body language. How far do these characters stand away from others? Are they focused on other people or distracted and looking at someone else?[24]

• Look for role models. Think about bosses you've had or others in your life who exemplify civility. On a piece of paper, list these people and describe what each does to help others feel respected. Then take a separate sheet of paper and divide it into two columns. Pick one of your role models, and in the first column, list episodes when that person cared the least about you and other members of your team; in the second column, list episodes when he or she cared the most about you and the other members of your team. Connect these specifics to outcomes. What did each action buy him or her?

With these tips in your back pocket, it won't be long before you become a genius at reading others' emotions. Your behavior will become more civil in turn.

Strategy #6: Make Time for Reflection

Keep a journal to provide insight into when, where, and why you are your best self and when, where, and why you are uncivil.[25] Identify people or situations that cause you to lose your temper. One leader I worked with, who began her day before 5:00 a.m., noticed that she became curt in the late afternoon, when she was tired and less attuned emotionally. Now she is much more mindful of her behavior. If she knows that she faces a challenging social situation or a situation that requires tact, she tries to postpone it until the following morning.

A journal also allows you to track your progress. After a week, a month, or three months, are you seeing your behavior become more civil? What is making the difference? How are others reacting to your behavior? Has anyone complimented you for behaviors you've worked on? Keep a record of nonverbals you receive from others. Are you receiving more smiles and fewer raised eyebrows? Do you detect less resistance from others, like you have more sway? Are you happier as a result of any shifts in behavior you've made? Note it!

Strategy #7: Take Care of Yourself

The most common reason people give for behaving poorly is the feeling of being overloaded or stressed.[26] So take better care of yourself, starting with the basics: good nutrition, sleep, and stress management. While this advice may sound obvious, most people don't manage their energy very well, and they stand to gain significantly from prioritizing it.

In a study I performed of over twenty thousand people, more than half reported being unhealthy or having a poor sense of well-being. Well over half failed to exercise more than two days a week for at least twenty minutes; nearly a quarter reported never exercising.

Kick exercise up a notch: People in my study who exercised three or more days a week felt a 14 percent greater sense of thriving at work as compared with those who didn't exercise. As we'll see later, a sense of thriving can help you deal better with uncivil behavior directed your way, and it also prevents you from behaving rudely.

The more you exercise, the more you build up your cognitive potential and dump the noise in your head that weighs you down. It also rids your body of toxins and wards off stress,[27] as well as makes you sharper, more attentive, and more mindful of your and others' actions.

Sleep is equally important. Even though 95 percent of people need seven to eight hours of sleep a day, a large-scale study found that almost 30 percent of Americans get fewer than six hours per day; among those in management roles at organizations, 40.5 percent get fewer than six hours.[28] Large studies from Korea, Finland, Sweden, and England produced similar findings, revealing inadequate sleep to be a global phenomenon.[29]

All of this is terrible news for civility. The ability to manage your thoughts, emotions, urges, and behavior—your self-control or self-regulation—relies disproportionately on the prefrontal cortex and amygdala regions of the brain.[30] Levels of brain glucose are particularly important in fueling activity in these areas,[31] and they are replenished during sleep.[32] The equation is simple: Inadequate sleep lowers brain glucose levels, which impairs self-regulation and self-control, which can produce more incivility.

Sleep deprivation can also lead to more misunderstandings and poorer reactions. Lack of sleep affects our ability to read others and judge intent.[33] If you're sleep deprived, you're more likely to misinterpret emotions on others' faces and their tone of voice.[34] You're also more prone to express your feelings in a more negative manner and tone of voice.[35] As if all this wasn't bad enough, lack of sleep is linked to frustration, hostility, anxiety, low levels of joviality,[36] lower levels of trust,[37] and more interpersonally inappropriate behavior.[38]

Lack of sleep is especially damaging in the workplace. Studies have linked low sleep quantity and poor sleep to workplace deviance, impatience, and unethical behavior.[39] Sleep deprivation has also been shown to hurt the relationship between leaders and their followers, and to diminish how much help people provide their coworkers. The worst part is that sleepy people may not even be aware of their negative impact on others.[40]

In addition to getting your needed sleep, please don't neglect nutrition.[41] Eating healthily keeps your glucose levels high, allowing you to tolerate difficult situations better—without blowing up. Think about it: How well do you respond to frustrations when you're famished?

During your workday, eat lightly but often to keep your blood glucose levels balanced. Shoot for a balance of 40 percent grains, 40 percent fruits and vegetables, and 20 percent protein-rich foods. Snacks (100 to 150 calories) that are low on the glycemic index, eaten periodically throughout the day, will also help keep your glucose balanced. Strategic snacks include fruits, vegetables, and protein (nuts, seeds, Greek yogurt, cottage or string cheese).[42]

In addition to exercising, sleeping, and eating right, I also advise cultivating a mindfulness practice, such as meditation or yoga. Mindfulness allows you to process situations more slowly and thoughtfully. It resets your body and refines your focus, putting you in a better place to respond well to others.[43] It can also help you keep calm when you're frustrated and primed to unload on someone.

The Duke University School of Medicine found that one hour of yoga a week decreased stress levels in the employees of Aetna (an insurance company) by a third. (It also reduced healthcare costs by an average of $2,000 per year!)[44] Other companies have benefitted as well. Janice Marturano was a senior in-house attorney at General Mills who helped lead the company through a brutal eighteen-month acquisition of Pillsbury.[45] Stressed out from that experience, as well as the death of both her parents, Marturano headed to a leadership retreat headed by Jon Kabat-Zinn, founder of the Center for Mindfulness in Medicine, Health Care, and Society. The weeklong transformative experience replenished her and greatly improved her self-awareness. She became a champion for mindfulness as a tool for her company's leaders and eventually all its employees. General Mills went on to introduce a Mindful Leadership program, as a result, as well as a seven-week mindfulness training course. Among senior executives who took the course, 80 percent reported improvements in their ability to make decisions and 89 percent reported becoming better listeners.[46]

Never Stop Learning

The best doctors, athletes, and business leaders really are constantly learning. They are humble enough to ask a colleague, coach, or trusted source to help them perform at their best. We can improve if we show a similar humility and take steps to improve our self-awareness. Armed with this information, we can begin tweaking our behavior to enhance our influence and effectiveness. Check in with teammates, friends, and family. Embrace feedback. Use it to get even better. But at the same time, don't feel you need to tackle all dimensions of your "bad" behavior at once. Start with the basics first.

In the next chapter, I'll cover some of the fundamentals we should all strive to master. These fundamentals will help you become the person you want to be, enhancing your influence and effectiveness along the way.

KEY POINTS

- Take the civility quiz. The online version (found at http://cycletocivility.com/) will provide customized feedback and suggestions.

- Collect feedback from others to discover your shortcomings and target improvements.

- Gather ideas on how to adjust specific behaviors.

- Enlist teammates or trusted sources to hold you accountable. Check in with them to gauge your progress.

- Take care of yourself to boost your chances for success. Managing your energy can help prime you for more effective interactions with others.

CHAPTER **6**

The Fundamentals

> Get the fundamentals down and the level of everything you
> do will rise.
>
> —Michael Jordan

In 2012, Tom Gardner, CEO of Motley Fool, an organization dedi-
cated to helping the world invest better, issued a challenge to his 250
employees. In order to get the 20 percent annual bonus the company
normally gave, each employee would have to know the name of every
other employee by year's end. If an employee couldn't name every
other person who worked at Motley Fool, he or she wouldn't get the
bonus. Further, Gardner explained that *all* employees would have to
name every employee by name for *anyone* to get the 20 percent.

A month before the end of the year, everyone but one person had
learned all the employees' names. This former Army Ranger wrote an
e-mail to all the other employees, saying, "I'm the last thing standing between you and your 20 percent bonus. Who wants to take me
to lunch?" People began reaching out to him, and before long, he
too could name everyone.

Gardner was trying to build stronger bonds between employees and to enhance the organization's broader culture. He could have issued a proclamation from on high: "Let's treat one another like family." He could have created general metrics around "collegiality" or "culture." Instead he realized that relationships came down to a few basic behaviors. In order to strengthen interactions between people, everyone should know one another by name.

Gardner might be onto something: Motley Fool racked up Glassdoor's number one culture rating for a small- to midsize organization once again in 2015. Remarkably, by industry standards, the company also boasts a turnover rate that is lower than 2 percent.[1]

To become more civil or help your organization build a more civil culture, you need to focus first on getting the basics right. You have to be attentive. You have to plug in. You have to smile more. These and other behaviors aren't rocket science. We all learned them in kindergarten. Yet we tend to forget them as we grow older. Our perspectives change and, with them, our habits. Before we know it, we're a long way from civil.

The following chapters—6 through 9—discuss several dimensions of civil behavior, including being inclusive, giving, and practicing e-civility. Do these things well, and you'll gain more influence and help everyone on your team deliver their best. But let's start with the low-hanging fruit, the small behaviors we frequently overlook that allow us to connect by our being attentive. Each of us can become more civil today by noticing how we behave from moment to moment and striving to behave just a little bit differently. I'm not asking you to adopt twenty behaviors, or even ten. For now, just think about doing *three* things differently. I promise you'll see a difference in how people respond to you and judge you.

Please and Thank You

Can simple gestures of civility really make a difference in the amount of influence we have? Absolutely. Duke University coach

Mike Krzyzewski shared an example from his time as assistant coach on the Olympics Dream Team, which won the gold medal in Barcelona in 1992. The team was loaded with superstars, but Michael Jordan was the best player. Jordan had donned the Carolina blue color of the University of North Carolina at Chapel Hill, which happened to be Duke's rival. On that count alone, "Coach K" wondered whether Jordan would show him respect as a coach. He also knew that although he enjoyed a certain amount of fame, he was nothing compared to Michael Jordan, who was a superstar and a living legend.

After the first practice, Jordan walked over to Coach K, who was drinking a soda. Coach K figured that Jordan was going to chide him for his Duke affiliation. He was shocked when Jordan said, "Coach, I'd like to work on some individual moves for about a half hour. Would you please work with me?" Coach K reported that they worked together, and at the end, Jordan warmly thanked him.[2]

Please and thank you—simple stuff, right? Yet these small actions made a tremendous impression on Coach K. In his own words,

Of all the things that I learned on that trip, that meeting was the most important. I still get chills thinking about it. Those kinds of events are force multipliers for any team. Jordan could have been the biggest prima donna in the world, but he wasn't. He understood that on that team there wasn't any totem pole, that everybody was important. He could have called out "Hey, Mike, get over here," and I would have run over there. And I would have felt like an idiot, but I would have done that job, and I would have lost respect for myself. He didn't want that, so he said, "Coach," and then he said, "Please," and at the end he said, "Thank you." How good is that? I think it was masterful on his part. It's a powerful thing when a person who is

in Jordan's position does things like that to create an environ-
ment that's conducive to success. I don't know if he knew he was
doing that, but he did it, and I respect him forever for it—and
it had a big impact on my own coaching back at Duke.[3]

To understand why small gestures of civility matter so much, let's consider what it is that usually makes people like us. Scholars around the world have studied more than two hundred behavior traits. Of these, it turns out that two in particular—warmth and competence—drive the impressions we make. That's it. These two qualities account for more than 90 percent of positive or negative impressions we form of the people around us.[4] If people see you as warm and competent, they're more inclined to trust you, build relationships with you, follow you, and support you.[5]

There's a catch, however: Strength in one of these traits typically implies weakness in the other. You've probably heard people say things like "He's very smart, but people won't like working for him" or "She's really friendly, but probably not all that bright."[6] Coach K thought Michael Jordan was a superstar but also a prima donna—in other words, competent but not warm.[7] But what if I told you there is one thing you can do that will show people you are both smart *and* friendly. You would do it, right? Well, there is: Be civil.[8]

If you want to connect with your employee or team, lead with warmth. Most of us are in a hurry to prove our competence,[9] but warmth contributes significantly more to others' evaluations. Warmth is the pathway to influence. It facilitates trust, information, and idea sharing. Even small nonverbals (e.g., a smile, a nod, or an open posture) invite people in, showing them that you're attentive to them and their needs.

Research in psychology and sociology suggests that by focusing on connecting with warmth and *then* integrating competence, you will improve your influence by establishing and enhancing your relationship bond.[10] For example, Princeton professor Alex Todorov and his colleagues have studied the cognitive and neural mechanisms that drive the snap judgments we make when looking at people's faces. Their research has shown that people consistently pick up on warmth faster than competence. We make these judgments in as little as thirty-three milliseconds![11] Not only are we quick when it comes to judging lack of warmth and incivility, but we're also unforgiving.[12] People feel that a single negative-warmth act or a single positive-competent act reveals character.

Warmth is so important because humans have a basic need to feel a sense of belonging and inclusion, what scientists call "affiliation."[13] Affiliation is one of our three most fundamental needs, along with autonomy and competence, and it's arguably the most important.[14] Neuroscientist Naomi Eisenberger and her colleagues suggest that our need for affiliation and inclusion is so strong that when we are ostracized, the very same neural regions in the brain light up that are activated in response to physical pain.[15] Social rejection can be literally "painful."

Conversely, by employing the three civility fundamentals that follow, you can connect with people in ways that highlight your warmth, satisfying others' need for affiliation. Meanwhile, you're also highlighting your competence by displaying social skills. Think of how smart, alert, competent, and in control Michael Jordan came across by saying please and thank you. Through civility, you demonstrate that you are mindful of others, willing to adhere to norms of respect, and able to regulate your behavior to comply with these specific norms.[16]

First Civility Fundamental: Smiling

The first civility fundamental is a behavior I'll bet you don't do nearly as much as you think, an act you've done since you were an infant, one that can instantly make you feel better even as it enhances your civility: *Smiling*.

Ever wonder why it's hard to resist smiling in the presence of happy children? Kids smile as often as four hundred times a day, but only 30 percent of adults smile more than twenty times a day, and 14 percent don't crack a smile five times a day.[17] That's tragic! If you fall into the majority of people who smile less than once an hour on average, then now is the time to start letting your inner child run wild.

The act itself of smiling lifts your mood, boosts your immune system, decreases stress, lowers blood pressure, and reduces your risk of heart attack.[18] One smile alone can provide the same level of brain stimulation as up to two thousand chocolate bars![19] Smiling is also associated with living longer.[20] A study that examined the baseball card photos of Major League players in 1952 found that the span of a player's smile predicted the length of his life. Broad smilers lived to an average age of seventy-nine, as opposed to seventy-two for those who didn't smile as much. Seven years more of life—just by smiling.

And smiling rubs off on others. Without saying a word, you can use it to put people at ease, build rapport, and inspire. Swedish researchers found that simply looking at a picture of a happy face can cause the muscles around our mouths to momentarily pull upward into a smile.[21] Many leadership coaches advise leaders to smile when talking on the phone because their voices will sound more positive and friendlier.

As motivational speaker Leo Buscaglia remarked, "Too often we underestimate the power of a touch, a smile, a kind word, a listening ear, an honest compliment, or the smallest act of caring, all of which have the potential to turn a life around."[22] When we smile we not only appear more likeable and courteous but are perceived to be more competent.[23] Scientists have also confirmed that smiling has the power to make people around us more effective. In one study of the US Navy, researchers evaluated the leaders of the most efficient, safest, and most highly prepared squadrons. These units turned out to be more positive and outgoing, more emotionally expressive and dramatic, warmer and more sociable. They were more appreciative and gentler than the leaders of average squadrons. And, yes, they smiled more.[24]

I've often observed the power of smiling in my own life. As a PhD student, I once attended a job talk for a professor whose work I admired. Job talks are part of the process by which a candidate applies for a faculty position. They are inherently stressful and can be downright nasty since existing faculty members often take the opportunity to challenge the candidate on his or her work. On this occasion, faculty members in the room pushed the candidate hard. A couple of times I looked at her, smiled, and nodded. I was trying to say "You got this." And she did. Later that afternoon, when this speaker met with a group of us PhD students, she explicitly and repeatedly thanked me for the smiles and nods. She has since gone on to be a terrific mentor to others and myself. That would have happened anyway, without my encouragement, but the smile certainly didn't hurt.

How do you get yourself to smile more? I'd recommend an "inside-out" approach, one grounded in both science and Method acting that involves purposely experiencing positive emotions internally and then naturally producing an authentic smile. Social psychologist Amy Cuddy describes the purposeful experience of emotion as "more like preparatory power posing: you're configuring your brain and body to smoothly and naturally perform well." The key is to figure out what you're doing when you're producing natural smiles; after all, almost everyone produces them naturally on some occasions. Just think about what makes you happy—maybe it's your kids or a favorite hobby or a joke someone told you—and then think about that when you want to smile.[25]

The alternative—trying to change the nonverbal behavior consciously, from the outside in—doesn't work so well. For most of us, "faking" a smile is hard to do. You see this all the time in politics. Some politicians who have a reputation for unfriendliness are coached to smile more often, yet their smiles are ill-timed—occurring when making a serious comment, when staring smugly at an opponent, or after tearing someone down. As a result, they come off as inauthentic. It's one thing to remember to smile; it's much harder to sync this up with other nonverbals, such as our tone and behaviors.[26]

If you're adopting the inside-out approach and you're in a pinch (as I sometimes am), try laughing at your predicament.[27] It works—trust me! Also, any time you face a high-stakes or difficult situation, it's especially helpful to think of things that make you happy just *before* you're "on" (e.g., before going on stage, getting up in front of a group, or interviewing). As author Malcolm Gladwell observed, "Emotions begin or end on your face."[28] When you smile, you get those positive biological effects. The key, again, is to figure out what naturally draws those emotions out. Just thinking about them will enable you to produce natural smiles, which will create a positive cycle of emotions and behaviors.

Second Civility Fundamental: Building Relationships with Subordinates

Relationships with people lower than you in an organization matter. In one study, the Center for Creative Leadership (CCL) found that the most important success factor for those holding the top three jobs in a large organization was "relationships with sub-ordinates."[29] According to a worldwide study conducted by Towers Watson, the greatest driver of engagement was whether workers felt their managers were genuinely interested in their well-being. Less than 40 percent of employees felt so engaged.[30]

To relate well with a subordinate, you first have to acknowledge him or her. That sounds simple, but I'm often surprised to hear how often leaders fail to acknowledge the people working beneath them. A former student of mine, Adam, had graduated at the top of his class and was a student officer, a natural leader extremely motivated to make a difference. He had accepted an offer from an investment bank in New York City, and he quickly made his mark there. On his own initiative, he redesigned some systems at the bank that resulted in much greater efficiencies. He attracted the notice of his superiors and quickly rose in the ranks. But then he met his match: an uncivil boss.

Adam's boss made belittling comments and sent stinging e-mails. But the worst thing of all, Adam reported, was how she failed to acknowledge him. Every day she blew by him and others in the hall without bestowing the slightest eye contact, the simplest nod, the least effusive hello. As for asking "How are you?"—forget about it. Despite his success in the organization, Adam wound up leaving a year later. He decided it wasn't worth staying.

Feeling acknowledged matters. In the briefest of moments, you have the power to lift people up and make their day. Fail to acknowledge them, and you make them feel small, potentially ruining their day. It's your choice, so make the right one. Practice the 10/5 Way mentioned in chapter 4: If you're within ten feet, make eye contact and smile. If you're within five feet, say hello.

In order to acknowledge someone personally, it helps to actually know who the person is. That's where the Motley Fool's bonus policy comes in. You, as a leader, can take more time to know the people working for you, but you can also implement policies that encourage managers and leaders company-wide to do so too. Motley Fool has a number of policies in place to help people in the company get to know one another. For instance, the company offers free ten-dollar Starbucks gift cards to employees with one catch: Fools must use the cards to treat a coworker—ideally one they don't know well—to a drink.[31] Gardner encourages employees to use these coffee dates to learn about one another's projects, identify best practices Fools use, and collaborate on challenges or ideas.

Motley Fool also tailors onboarding policies to help existing and new employees get to know one another well. Before new Fools start, Motley Fool sends them a questionnaire asking about their favorite things (foods, sports, movies, vacation spots, etc.), investing experience, and more. When they arrive, their desk is decked out with favorite items. A new Fool who loves traveling may get a scratch-off map or a book about the best places in the world to visit. This not only is fun for the new Fool but also gives others a snapshot of the Fool's personality and helps to identify mutual interests.

Plus, the new Fool's manager calls him or her before their first day to offer congratulations and answer any questions. On a Fool's first day, which is always a Friday, he or she receives a First Day Survival Kit, filled with UNO cards, Silly Putty, candy, and a NERF gun. He or she also receives an office tour led by a Leadership Fool to highlight the company's high-performance culture; has lunch with Fools outside their department to make connections; and participates in a team party. On the Fool's second day, he or she meets a Fool Buddy, a tenured Fool who will regularly check in to answer questions about the company, culture, or processes. At New Fool Coffees—monthly events at the company's headquarters—recent hires can spend an hour with the founders, learning more about the company and asking questions.[32]

Third Civility Fundamental: Listening

Listening well is essential for creating, maintaining, and deepening relationships; it signals caring, commitment, and connection.

Listening can also yield vital information and insights. If employees don't believe their bosses are listening, they're far less likely to offer ideas and helpful suggestions.[33] They're also more likely to become emotionally exhausted and to quit.[34] Yet listening is hard work, requiring both energy and concentration. Just think of all that you might do during any given social interaction *instead* of listening. You might interrupt the speaker, one-upping him or her with an account of your own experiences. You might chime in with unsolicited advice. Or you might pretend to listen but actually tune out, jumping to conclusions about what you think the speaker will say next or rehearsing what you're going to say next.

How can you listen better? I've posed this question to people the world over. No matter the place or culture, the answer is the same: Be there completely. Make a list beforehand of questions or topics you want to cover to prevent brain freeze.[35] Get into the moment with the person facing you. Dump distractions; try to clear your mind of all of them.[36] Put your phone away and put your blinders on. Focus all your attention. Join in on the conversation in the fullest sense. At its core, civility is about connecting in a human way with others. We don't connect by passively hearing. We connect by taking in everything the other person is sharing with us.

Also, make eye contact. Match your expressions to the speaker's emotions. Rather than judging a speaker, focus on the emotion as well as the content of what they're saying. Focus also on what they're not saying. Be patient. Paraphrase what you hear to show understanding, but don't interrupt with new points. Use pauses to reflect or draw out more information.[37] Ask clarifying questions to improve the focus of the conversation.[38] You might take notes to stay focused while listening.

Julian Treasure, an expert on conscious listening, suggests keeping in mind a useful acronym: RASA. *Receive* by paying attention to the person; *Appreciate* by making little noises, such as "Oh";

Summarize what the other person said (e.g., "So, in your opinion, you think..."); and *Ask* questions afterward.[39]

Do you practice any or all of these four principles? In general, how completely or selectively do you listen? Do you tune out some people based on their status, skills, intelligence, gender, or cultural background? Does the setting or situation make a difference? Do certain triggers cause you to stop listening? For example, when a conversation turns negative or you must deal with unpleasant information, do you stop listening?

Be sure also to probe more deeply into your behaviors when engaging in conversations with others. Do you interrupt with your own ideas? Do you change the subject frequently and steer it to something that interests you more? Do you get defensive when others don't agree on your stance on a topic? Do you argue? Does your mind wander during a conversation so you need something repeated? Do you talk more than you listen?

I struggle with many of these behaviors. The key is to become more mindful of them. Work on your shortcomings. If you have the urge to interrupt, as I often do, stop yourself from jumping into the conversation before the other person completes his or her thoughts. Over time, restraining yourself will feel more natural. You'll relax and no longer feel the need to monitor yourself as closely. You'll get used to waiting it out—even patiently! As we discussed in the previous chapter, ask friends or colleagues to help coach you on this, providing feedback and calling you out when you revert to interrupting.

Nearly fifteen years ago, I had a friend and colleague, Peter, who noticed my inkling to dive in and finish his or others' thoughts. If there was a pregnant pause in our conversation, I was happy to help Peter along, finish his thoughts, or insert my question. On a number of occasions, he kindly but directly called me out. I found myself looking at the ground, completely embarrassed. While my urge to jump in hasn't disappeared, my self-control has improved.

If you like to talk or if you struggle to share the floor, ask others what *they* think more often. It's one of the most powerful questions a leader can ask. A junior surgeon used this question brilliantly, engaging people with less status who might otherwise have refrained from speaking. He coaxed them to share, and they loved it.

Think about what probing or clarifying questions you might humbly ask. Then listen. In meetings, ask someone to monitor your actions and record your questioning-to-informing ratio. The ratio should be at least two to one. These fundamentals of civility are extremely effective. Remember, people desperately want to connect, to be heard and seen and understood.[40] Others feel you care if you master these three fundamentals, which are all tied to being attentive and connecting. Don't forget to smile. It's an amazing tool that benefits you and others. Acknowledge others, and master listening. Focus on being fully present, listening with open ears and an open heart. Make the effort to acknowledge people and develop relationships with employees and teammates. That's at the core of civil behavior.

KEY POINTS

- At its core, civility is about connecting in a human way with others. What are you doing to connect with people?

- Civility is so important because it conveys both warmth and competence.

- Before addressing other aspects of civility, master the basics: smile more, acknowledge people, and listen effectively.

CHAPTER 7

Judge Not

Be civil to all, sociable to many, familiar with few, friend to one, enemy to none.

—Benjamin Franklin

In the spring of 2013, when Argentinian archbishop Jorge Bergoglio was selected to succeed Pope Benedict as leader of the Catholic Church, he struck a decidedly new tone.[1] Breaking with tradition, he dressed in a simple white robe when addressing the crowds at Saint Peter's Square.[2] He decided on the name Pope Francis, after the humble friar Saint Francis of Assisi, who had chosen to live in poverty and serve the poor.[3] At mass, he sat among the cardinals as opposed to sitting on a large throne above them. He chose to live in more modest accommodations inside the Vatican guesthouse rather than in the opulent Vatican palace, so he would be physically closer to the people.[4]

Bergoglio's message wasn't one of only humility but also acceptance, tolerance, and the need for Catholics to refrain from judgment. Long before he became pope, Bergoglio had challenged

Catholics to forge bonds with people in need and of different faith traditions. During his first Wednesday general audience in Saint Peter's Square, Pope Francis urged people "to come out of ourselves, to go to meet others, to go toward the peripheries of life, to be the first to move toward our brothers and sisters, especially the ones who are far away, forgotten, who most need understanding, consolation, help." On Maundy (Holy) Thursday, he became the first pope in history to wash and kiss the feet of two Muslims at the juvenile detention center Casal del Marmo in Rome.[5]

Bergoglio's nonjudgmental stance hardly ended there. On one occasion, when confronted with a question about gays and lesbians in the Church, he responded quite strikingly, "Who am I to judge?"[6] He also proclaimed a Year of Mercy, encouraging Catholics to "open wide" their hearts in forgiveness and reach out to others who have upset them. Although Catholics seeking to be cleansed of their sins typically have to trek to the Holy Door in Rome to receive absolution, Pope Francis declared that the doors would be open in all dioceses around the world, as well as in prisons.[7]

Such values of inclusion, openness, and acceptance matter in the workplace too. It's well known that diversity adds value to organizations,[8] allowing groups to perform better, make smarter decisions, and be more innovative and organizations to drive market growth.[9] Diverse organizations that welcome everyone possess greater insights into the marketplace. Diversity is also a valuable recruiting tool that helps organizations land top talent. In a recent Glassdoor survey, two-thirds of people polled reported that diversity was important to them when evaluating companies and job offers.[10]

Yet diversity alone can't provide the benefits we seek. Diversity's true value depends on teammates' culture and attitudes. If incivility reigns and people feel as though they aren't valued, or they lack permission to speak up and share opinions, they won't contribute. Diversity, in turn, will mean little. People need to feel *respected* in order to contribute. And that's where civility comes in. We must treat *everyone* well, including individuals who are different from ourselves or think differently. Data shows that true inclusion is quite difficult for most people.[11] Even if we consciously want to, we have a hard time welcoming others in. In fact, we show unconscious bias, often through subtle attitudes or actions. Let's take a look at unconscious bias and explore how you and your organization can treat people in a more inclusive, respectful way.

Shortcuts That Hurt

We might meet people who are different from us and think to ourselves that we not only accept these individuals, we *like* them. And yet, underneath the surface, we perhaps still maintain certain perceptions about them based on their identity. Why? How come we can't shake these judgments?

The answer has to do with cognitive overload. Our minds are constantly bombarded with information—eleven million bits of information per second at any given time—yet our conscious minds are able to process only forty bits per second.[12] Therefore, the vast majority of information we take in is processed in an unconscious way. To cope, our brains take shortcuts, often relying on stereotypes as a way of filtering out unimportant or wrongheaded notions. Although these shortcuts help us to make quick decisions with limited information, they also lead us astray, since they cause us to treat others in a biased way.[13]

We assume, without even realizing it, that the older guy we see in a meeting has a poor memory or isn't nearly as creative.[14] We presume that the middle-aged woman driving a minivan would never be able to keep up in the boardroom—even though she might be fully capable of such a task. We suppose that the young guy in the wheelchair can't do much, and we are shocked to learn that he was a captain in the US Army and led thousands of troops until just a few months earlier.

Like many people, I've been a victim of unconscious bias. When I transferred into an elite private high school before my sophomore year, a guidance counselor met with my parents and me about my class load. She made several direct comments about my supposed inability to keep up with the school's "elite students." She didn't use the term "dumb jock," but it was pretty clear that was how she saw me. Not only was I a "jock," but I was also coming from a public high school with supposedly lower standards. I was bucketed as someone who couldn't handle honor classes—not there.

Later, when I began teaching undergraduate students, I didn't see athletes as dumb jocks or public school kids as less challenged, prepared, or capable. I could relate to the athletes; I knew what they were going through, and I admired them for their dedication and ability to balance academics and sports. And yet, I knew I still needed to manage my biases so I didn't end up ignoring the *non*-athletes. If I didn't watch out, my prior victimization at the hands of unconscious bias would take me down a path of incivility. And when that happens, it can prove costly indeed. Left unchecked, our unconscious biases can lead to inequalities in the workplace as well as low group performance.[15] As managers, we may miss out on choosing some of the best and brightest people for our teams, or we may evaluate performance and provide feedback in ways that hurt rather than help.

Research shows, for instance, that both men and women are more likely to shield women from unpleasant or embarrassing news by telling white lies.[16] Many people do this unknowingly, because they grew up thinking of women as fragile beings in need of protection and special treatment. But white lies are not harmless. If women don't get the same honest feedback that men do, they can fail to develop themselves as quickly or as effectively as they might, and their careers can suffer. Women say they *want* honest feedback, and they feel resentful if they detect that someone was lying about their performance.[17] Originating in assumptions that many women might find deeply offensive, white lies can do a whole lot of damage.

Unconscious biases around racial differences can cause similar problems. One law firm brought me in to teach their employees how to give more direct feedback. An African American related that, in his view, minorities weren't getting honest feedback because (again) colleagues felt as though they needed to be "protected" from it. Other partners backed him up. If we treat people as less than what they are capable of, we not only insult them but also set them up for failure. We make them into smaller versions of themselves, and as they start to lower their own expectations, failure becomes a self-fulfilling prophecy. We all lose out.

The first step in fighting unconscious bias is to make an effort to bring silent assumptions out into the open. Ask yourself, "What biases do I carry?" "Whom does that affect?" "What are the consequences?"

Like many people, you might acknowledge the phenomenon of unconscious bias yet doubt that you actually partake in it: "Others harbor biases," you say, "but not me! My mom worked, so I'm not biased against women in the workplace. I have Muslim and African American friends, so I'm clearly not biased against people of those backgrounds."[18]

If you doubt that you harbor biases, I challenge you to take the Implicit Association Test, a simple, five-minute, scientifically based exercise that cuts through your conscious mind to show you what happens below the surface. This test measures unconscious bias across a variety of categories: race, weight, disability, age, sexuality, gender, and more. The test is deceptively simple: You just sort two categories of words into left or right buckets as quickly as you can. Are you ready? Here is part of the test (the link for the full test is located in the Recommended Resources section) :

Round 1

	Male	Female
Bucket the following:		
Husband	☐	☐
Uncle	☐	☐
Grandpa	☐	☐
Son	☐	☐
Boy	☐	☐
Girl	☐	☐
Mother	☐	☐
Daughter	☐	☐
Grandma	☐	☐
Wife	☐	☐

Round 2

	Liberal Arts	Science
Bucket the following:		
Engineering	☐	☐
Biology	☐	☐
Music	☐	☐
Chemistry	☐	☐

	Female or Liberal Arts	Male or Science
Literature	☐	☐
Geology	☐	☐
English	☐	☐
Humanities	☐	☐
Physics	☐	☐
Math	☐	☐

Round 3

	Female or Liberal Arts	Male or Science
Bucket the following:		
Music	☐	☐
Mother	☐	☐
Philosophy	☐	☐
Father	☐	☐
History	☐	☐
Wife	☐	☐
Engineering	☐	☐
Son	☐	☐
Chemistry	☐	☐
Physics	☐	☐

Round 4

Bucket the following:	Male or Liberal Arts	Female or Science
Father	☐	☐
Engineering	☐	☐
Music	☐	☐
Daughter	☐	☐
Uncle	☐	☐
Math	☐	☐
Girl	☐	☐
Literature	☐	☐
Husband	☐	☐
Physics	☐	☐

About 75 percent of people who have taken this test online complete it faster when females are sorted with liberal arts studies, not science; when white faces are sorted alongside pleasant words; and when male terms are sorted alongside career terms.[19] It matters little whether you're white or black, a woman or a man, old or young. Unconscious bias is real, and we are all more biased than we think.

This means we all have work to do to curb the unconscious bias in our daily lives. We must question our perceptions on a minute-by-minute basis when we engage with others, consciously correcting for our improper assumptions. Awareness is the crucial first step. Reflect on your tendencies. What experiences have colored your perceptions, and how?

As social neuroscientists Jay van Bavel and Will Cunningham have shown, an effective strategy for limiting unconscious bias is to take a moment to focus on similarities and common identities. In their initial experiments, Bavel and Cunningham gave participants a word-sorting task, asking them to quickly categorize words as "good" or "bad." Before each word, they briefly showed the face of a white or black male. Participants revealed typical unconscious bias: They saw white faces as positive, but not black faces.

Then the researchers took a separate set of participants through the same task. But before the task began, Bavel and Cunningham showed them the faces and told them that some of the white and black faces belonged to students who would be on their team during a later task, while the other faces were from the opposing team. Participants showed the same positive bias toward black faces of fellow team members that other participants had previously shown only for whites. Knowing someone is a member of their team erased the unconscious biases.[20]

Think about your connections with people. List what you have in common with someone, however different he or she seems to be. Emphasize your shared identity as parents, as residents of a city, as fans of a sports team, as members of a religious community, etc.[21] It's human nature to feel positively toward members of our own group, so the key is to find a shared identity or group.

Also, audit your hiring and promotion decisions.[22] Have you hired a disproportionate number of members of your race lately? If so, you might try switching it up. You might also try exposing yourself to environments that challenge your biases.[23] My uncle, Terence Clark, does this through interfaith work in the San Francisco Bay Area (and for decades working on racial issues in the Cleveland area) in which people from Christian, Muslim, Jewish, and other faiths come together to engage in dialogue and activities. Biases are reduced when we learn about one another through personal interaction. There is also a promotion of goodwill and, as this becomes regular practice, a growing support for one another.[24]

Try providing structure or routines in areas like hiring, performance evaluations, and promotion decisions that prevent unconscious biases from creeping in. Make it a point to slow down, weigh all the evidence, and remove subjectivity from the process. Finally, combat your biases by including others' opinions. For important work decisions, use committees. Research shows that teams with divergent opinions tend to make better, less-biased decisions.[25]

Google's Journey

As Google has proven, it's also possible to tackle unconscious biases on an organizational level.[26] Google understood well the value of diversity but felt it needed a culture that openly supported diversity and addressed unconscious biases. Google executives thus asked themselves three questions:

1. How can we raise collective awareness about the power of our unconscious biases?
2. What are the decisions we're making every day, and how can we unbias them?
3. Can we create and sustain a culture shift?[27]

To tackle unconscious bias, Google first had to overcome diversity's most common barrier: denial. A typical employee might have thought, *Unconscious bias here? Never.* In addition to taking the Implicit Association Test, Google employees were shown research that revealed systemic bias in the workplace.[28] In one study, for instance, researchers found that men who pitched ideas to venture capitalists were 60 percent more likely to get their ideas funded than women (their chances got even better if they were good-looking).[29]

Employees also learned about the unseen power of unconscious bias. In one study uncovered by Google executives, researchers modeled the effects of unconscious biases in a fictitious organization with eight levels.[30] There were five hundred employees at level one and ten employees at level eight.[31] The researchers assumed 15 percent attrition at every level per year. Employees who left the company were replaced by employees from the level below based on their performance scores. The researchers were quite conservative in programming performance score differences; women's performance scores were calculated to be just 1 percent less than men's scores. Yet after nineteen years, only 38 percent of the employees at level eight were women. Even tiny, seemingly insignificant gender biases with performance ratings can affect advancement decisions dramatically over time, shaping an organization's overall composition.[32]

Studies like this helped convince many Google employees that their unconscious biases not only existed but mattered.[33] The challenge now was what to do about it. The research in psychology and related fields offered few ideas for how to conquer unconscious biases, and little evidence existed suggesting that any particular approach worked. Still, Google executives were undeterred (as per usual).

They decided first to educate their employees about unconscious bias. The company's People Operations team developed a voluntary sixty- to ninety-minute training program called Unconscious Bias @ Work. The content featured external research (including studies I've mentioned) as well as internal examples of Google's efforts to conquer unconscious bias.[34] (For more about the training program, see the Recommended Resources section.) As of 2016, more than thirty thousand of Google's fifty-five thousand employees have gone through the program. Google studied its effects and found that program participants were significantly more aware of unconscious bias, had greater understanding of it, and were more motivated to overcome it.[35] Just one month after attending the workshop, participants were more likely to perceive Google's culture as fair, objective, and attuned to diversity than those in the control group.[36]

In addition to the training, Google has imposed structured interviews to prevent unconscious biases from entering into hiring decisions.[37] Managers are also given a "bias busting" checklist of assumptions, so they are more aware during business decisions and processes. Every six months, as managers meet to assess employees on performance, they receive this checklist and are encouraged to consider specific behaviors and the situations that trigger them. Managers are also encouraged to use the checklist to test themselves and to call out executives and employees whenever they see them succumb to unconscious biases.

Unbiasing Checklists for Performance Review Conversations[38]	
Action	**Biases Targeted**
Communicate the performance expectations for your employee in that role and level	Stereotype-based Biases
Make sure cited feedback and examples come from the entire assessment period	Recency Bias
Discuss important work that may not have been visible	Availability Bias
Differentiate between situational factors (in the workplace) and personal factors that affected performance	Fundamental Attribution Error
Use multiple concrete, behavioral examples from reviewers to support both strengths and development areas	Leniency Error, Self-Serving Bias
Imagine your direct report in a different social group and ask yourself whether your feedback would be the same	Stereotype-Based Biases

Most notably, Google encourages managers and employees to examine their own unconscious biases and to call out the biases of others when they see them. I once witnessed firsthand Google employees calling out hidden biases when I attended an event at the company. Over lunch, our conversation drifted to a woman who had recently had a baby. I made a comment about being really happy about the work flexibility Google offered so she could care for her newborn. In a kind, playful way, a Google employee shouted, "Implicit bias! Implicit bias!" Guilty as charged. Yes, I was carrying certain perceptions of working women that do not hold true for others. Had the story been about a male colleague, my mind wouldn't have wandered to *How is he going to balance it all? What will his new work arrangement be? Maybe his working years are over...* or, worse, *He won't be able to handle it all at once.*

I was embarrassed, but fortunately the type of alert I received from the Google employee made me aware of my bias. In the future, my chances of making a similar comment will be that much lower.

Start the Conversation

Other organizations have also started their journeys to inclusion, and as their experiences reveal, so much can be accomplished by simply starting a conversation. In 2015, Expedia's vice president of inclusion strategies Britta Wilson conducted a world tour of the company's facilities, hosting events to promote dialogue and understanding about inclusion. Although inclusion had been absent from the company's vocabulary just nine months earlier, it was cited as Expedia's most positive attribute in the company's recent employee engagement survey. As Wilson told me, employees are gleaning a better understanding of what it means to create and participate in a workplace of respect, of trust, of equity of access, and with the opportunity for all to wholly engage. More important, they are now open to having new kinds of conversations. Now when employees believe they have experienced a slight related to unconscious bias, they are much more likely to talk about it instead of letting it eat away at them. Civility 1, Incivility 0.

Wilson was recently in one of Expedia's global offices to give a town hall talk on inclusion. After the meeting, a couple of female employees reported feeling that the men in the office were talking down to them. Several male employees then responded that they didn't intend to demean or diminish their female colleagues; they were simply brought up with certain preconceived notions of "the female role." In one instance shared by the women, while the team continued to work through a complex problem late into the day, the male team leader turned to the female on the team and said, "We can finish up here, so that you can go home to prepare dinner for your husband and children." The female retorted, "Don't worry, I have that covered." The male employee thought he was being kind and thoughtful; he found it perfectly acceptable that his female colleague might have to leave, and he had only been trying to give her permission to do so. The team then had a lively discussion regarding their rules of engagement. As Wilson related, these employees wouldn't have had a productive conversation about this kind of encounter if the company hadn't initiated and nurtured discourse around inclusion.

Beyond sponsoring formal conversations like Expedia does, look for fun and creative ways to bring employees together. At SpaceX, a divide exists between hourly and full-time workers, and also between technical employees designing the cool rockets and other employees. To bridge these divides, the company has devised an experiment called Lunchtime Roulette. SpaceX buys lunch, inviting a group of workers from across the company to eat together and explore common interests. So far, the program seems effective, and research would suggest that the company will see improved collaboration and, with it, performance gains.

Pope Francis has it right: The judgments we make about people don't help; they hurt. We must work hard to open up, in both our own lives and the organizations in which we work. To reap the full benefits of civility, we must come to grips with the often unconscious ways we diminish others. Follow Pope Francis's example: Be respectful and treat others as equals at every moment. In doing so, you will enable your colleagues to realize their full potential, even as you realize your own.

KEY POINTS

- All of us carry unconscious biases into our thoughts and interactions with others.

- Think about what biases you may hold and how this affects your interactions.

- Raise awareness about unconscious biases with your teams, and talk openly about the incorrect assumptions you're making and why they might hurt others.

CHAPTER **8**

Give More

The wise man does not lay up his own treasures. The more he gives to others, the more he has for his own.

—Lao Tzu

Once you have the fundamentals of civility in place, take your game to the next level. Let's look a little closer at one of the basics of civility: smiling. What are you really doing when you smile at someone? You might pass a colleague in the hallway and simply nod your head and continue on, but when you smile instead, you convey to that person the basic pleasure you feel at having crossed paths. For a brief moment, you offer an expression of warmth and fellow feeling. You don't *have* to offer it; nobody is forcing you. Yet you do, of your own volition. And by smiling back, your colleague returns the favor.

To master civility at work, we need to give many things, not just smiles. Based on my research and consulting experience, I've identified five forms of giving that are especially important for building an atmosphere of kindness and respect. Master these five forms, and you'll create a wonderful ripple effect, inducing those around you to give as well. As the Greek statesman Pericles once said, "What you leave behind is not what is engraved in stone monuments but what is woven into the lives of others." What you leave behind is what you give.

Share Resources

To increase your civility, share the tools, knowledge, social contacts, and time at your disposal. I can already hear the objections: In our ultra-competitive world, who can *afford* to share his or her scarce resources? Isn't that overly idealistic?

Not at all! In his bestseller *Give and Take*, Wharton School professor Adam Grant describes how giving in the business world can leave the giver with actually more, not less. At first, and in most contexts, giving seems inefficient. In sales, for instance, givers may put their customers' need for a better price above their own need to hit a sales target. In medical schools, students may invest time and energy in helping their friends, leaving less time for themselves to focus and study. Yet Grant found that after a year in sales, generous people achieved the highest revenues, and by the end of medical school, students who had helped others attained top grades.[1]

What explains these results? Two things: better relationships and motivation. As Grant reveals, givers build deeper and broader connections that remain intact over time, which pays off. Sharing resources also provides givers with a sense of meaning and purpose, energizing them to do more—they feel their contributions matter, so when the going gets tough, they don't give up.[2]

My research reveals similar benefits. In a study of more than four hundred employees of an international consulting firm, my colleagues and I found that the highest performers shared more than twice as many resources with coworkers than their average or lowest performing colleagues did.[3] Sharing not only elicited a feel-good response but also enhanced productivity. This finding held irrespective of the amount of resources high sharers had originally received.

Of course, you must be smart about how much and what exactly you give. Across more than three hundred organizations, Rob Cross, Reb Rebele, and Adam Grant found that up to a third of value-added collaborations come from only 3 to 5 percent of employees.[4] In other words, some people in organizations are giving a lot—and possibly too much. Cross, Rebele, and Grant noted the importance of distinguishing between the three types of collaborative resources that employees share with one another to create value: informational, social, and personal.[5] Informational resources refer to expertise that can be passed on. Social resources include one's awareness, access, and position in a network, all of which can be used to help colleagues better collaborate. Personal resources primarily involve one's time and energy. Informational and social resources can be shared efficiently, often in a single exchange; the giver also retains them. Personal resources, however, are finite and tend to deplete someone, leaving him or her with less time or energy.

While we often receive personal resource requests (e.g., a thirty-minute meeting invite), passing along information or making a personal introduction might also fulfill the needs of the person making the request.[6] It's worth using a little discretion when dispensing personal resources, particularly since some requests are a burden. This advice applies especially to women, since they tend to bear more of a burden and experience more emotional exhaustion.[7] A 2013 *Huffington Post* poll of Americans asked people to report on how often they contribute to others. Men were 36 percent more likely to share knowledge and expertise (an informational resource), while women were 66 percent more likely to help others in need (which typically requires more time and energy).[8] Consider whether you should shift the resources you give.

Of course, if you're like 95 percent of people, you aren't giving too much, and you'd stand to benefit from offering more to those around you. What connections might you make between people in your network? What information might you share that would help a friend or colleague? What could you contribute to your community based on your personal mission and interests? What small gestures of kindness might you bestow upon others? Have you told your friends or mentors lately how much they mean to you? Try to do more of these things, and pay attention to how your behaviors affect your emotions, spirit, mind, and body.

Share Recognition

Also, look for ways to give credit to everyone who helped you earn any kind of recognition, even if you deserve the lion's share. As scholar and author Warren Bennis has noted, good leaders shine under the spotlight, but great leaders help others shine.[9]

This kind of humility pays off in a number of ways. In a series of studies, researchers Bradley Owens, Michael Johnson, and Terence Mitchell showed that humility—which includes appreciating others' strengths and contributions—predicted individual performance beyond many personality characteristics and general mental ability.[10] Humble leaders fostered teams that were more focused on learning; their employees were more engaged, more satisfied with their jobs, and more likely to stay with their organization.[11] IBM's 2013/2014 WorkTrends survey of more than nineteen thousand workers revealed that engagement among employees who receive recognition is almost three times higher than among those who do not. Those who receive recognition are also far less likely to quit.[12]

Have you had the joy of working for a leader who generously lavished you with credit, even when he didn't need to? How did that feel? In one law firm I worked with, a partner made a point of acknowledging the work of his associates and paralegals, mentioning the specific information, leads, and ideas they generated. This partner was beloved; his employees would have run through a wall for him.

They were happy to put in extra hours when called upon, and others at the firm were begging to join his team. Plus, his subordinates were motivated enough to develop their own talents, further benefitting the organization. I've seen this pattern emerge dozens of times.

What might you do to share credit and promote others' work? What success stories might you share?

Research has shown that small wins can boost motivation and performance, so be sure to celebrate them along the way.[13] At the end of each meeting at Zingerman's, a Michigan-based company of food businesses, managers and employees take time to recognize one another.[14] Each month an employee is featured for exceptional service in the "Service Stars!" section of their newsletter and awarded fifty dollars. Employees who go beyond the call of duty are featured in the X-tra Mile Files of the newsletter.[15] Who can you high-five for their work or effort today? What's holding you back from giving someone a pat on the back?

Share Gratitude

Have you ever been thanked in a way that blew you away? My friend and coauthor Tony Schwartz likes to tell others about a time when he was a young journalist at the *New York Times*. Tony was talking on the phone one morning when a fast-rising editor walked by his desk, picked up a blank pad of paper, and wrote, "Yours is the best story in the paper today." Even decades later, he still thinks about it.[16] I had a similar memorable experience: A dean at a college where I was teaching handwrote a thank-you note and slipped it under my door after I had done an interview on *Fox News*. I was shocked to find it the next morning.

A simple, handwritten note can make all the difference. Saying thank you sets you apart. Do you know that most people thank their coworkers once a year at most?[17] Once a year! Adam Grant and

Francesca Gino found that a simple thank you from a supervisor improved employees' sense of self-worth, enhanced their confidence, and led to greater trust and willingness to help others.[18]

In one study, Grant and Gino asked participants to help a student improve a job application letter. After they had sent the student their feedback, the student replied with a message that read, "I just wanted to let you know that I received your feedback on my cover letter," and then went on to ask for help with another one. Only 32 percent of the participants helped the student. However, when the student added eight words, "Thank you so much! I am really grateful," the rate more than doubled—to 66 percent. In a separate study, after participants helped one student, another student followed up and asked for help. Being thanked by the first student more than *doubled* helping rates—from 25 percent to 55 percent. Your thanks may not only help you get what you want at work but help teammates get what they want too.[19]

Feeling genuinely appreciated lifts people up. It energizes. It's also a powerful tool for encouraging the right behaviors. If you really want to score points, keep in mind that every person has his or her own preferred ways of receiving gratitude for positive behaviors. Some of us like to bask in the limelight, while others dread that. Some of us like a verbal thank you; others prefer a gift or a kind gesture, such as flowers left on a desk, tickets to see their favorite team play, or a similar favor proffered in return. Take the time to notice what your employees prefer—or, even better, ask them directly. It will make them feel like you genuinely care about their success. Meanwhile, you're more likely to enhance others' trust in you, improve your relationships, and ultimately raise your income.[20] It's true: Grateful people earn about 7 percent more than their ungrateful colleagues.[21] They also experience lower stress, are more resilient and physically fit, have 12 percent lower blood pressure, and simply feel better.[22]

Share Feedback

Zingerman's decided to focus on sharing something many of us don't: feedback about performance. For them, this wasn't about only personal performance feedback but organizational performance as well. Over five years, Zingerman's implemented weekly gatherings around a whiteboard during which teams tracked results and forecasted the upcoming week's numbers. These metrics went beyond dollars and cents to include service and food-quality measures, sales averages, internal satisfaction figures, and "fun" (which could be anything from weekly contests to customer satisfaction ratings to employees' ideas for innovation). Sharing feedback has greatly increased Zingerman's frontline employees' sense of ownership, contributing to better performance. Between 2000 and 2010, the company's revenue has grown by almost 300 percent; its leaders credit their "open book management" as a key factor in that success.[23]

If you manage others, help your reports feel valued by giving them regular knowledge and updates on how the business is doing. Create a compelling scoreboard that highlights top priorities or important goals and, more specifically, the current situation (where you are now), the target result (where you need to be), and the deadline (by when). Encourage employees to review this scoreboard every day or every week, as appropriate. In meetings, highlight progress and ask your team to brainstorm possibilities on how to further achieve priorities.

Don't forget to give feedback on personal performance as well. Negative or directive feedback provides guidance, leading people to become, over time, more certain about their behavior and more confident in their competence.[24] To facilitate direct communication, some organizations have a code or sign they use to shift people into a "safe space," where they can more comfortably share unpleasant information. When people need to say something very direct at a Johnson & Johnson office, they pull a stuffed moose from the conference room shelf and put it on the table to symbolize no holding back or sugarcoating.

Specifically highlighting an employee's strengths can help generate a sense of accomplishment and motivation to continue that person's progress. The highest performers offer more positive feedback with their peers; in fact, high-performing teams share *six times* more positive feedback than average teams.[25] Meanwhile, low-performing teams share twice as much negative feedback than average teams. A Gallup survey found that 67 percent of employees whose managers focused on their strengths were fully engaged in their work, as compared with only 31 percent of employees whose managers focused on their weaknesses.[26]

The key to providing positive feedback is to do it in the moment, catching people just as they do things right. Which of your team members' positive contributions do you currently take for granted? Make a list, and start calling out team members for their strengths when you see them in action. The more specific you are, the better. And the more you notice what's meaningful to a person, the greater your potential impact. Some people enjoy receiving high fives in the moment in front of everyone; others prefer a pat on the back in private. Individuals may also feel especially proud of specific projects they've been working on or outcomes they've achieved; try to recognize these efforts if possible. Bring together positive and negative feedback by thinking about what you want each member of your team to start, stop, and continue doing. See if you can list a few straightforward actions for each of these prompts—and then share them.

If feedback truly is a gift, several steps can make it even more powerful and productive. Try to identify with the recipient of feedback and understand the emotions he or she is feeling. Explain the reason for the feedback, striving to be straightforward and honest. Imagine you are giving yourself the feedback: How would *you* want to hear it? And make sure to focus on the future: What can your employee do to move forward?

Also, as we discussed in chapter 5, pay attention to your facial expressions when you deliver feedback. Researcher Marie Dasborough observed two groups, one whose members received negative feedback accompanied by positive emotional signals (e.g., nods and smiles) and the other whose members received positive feedback delivered critically (e.g., with frowns and narrowed eyes).[27] Interviews Dasborough performed revealed that people who had received positive feedback accompanied by negative emotional signals reported feeling worse about their performance than participants who received good-natured negative feedback.[28] So always remember: The *delivery* of feedback can often be more important than the message itself.

Share Purpose

How does your work contribute beyond your immediate circle of colleagues and your organization? How do you improve or inspire the lives of others? How do you bring people together for mutual gain? Most people want to do meaningful work, but too many believe their efforts don't make a difference. That's too bad: Having a sense of meaning at work encourages personal growth,[29] work engagement,[30] and well-being.[31] Instilling others' work with a sense of meaning also carries benefits, increasing a sense of thriving and performance for that person while also cultivating stronger, deeper relationships.[32]

Any employee can lend meaning to the work of others. However, Adam Grant's research shows that the best source of inspiration comes from end users—the people who benefit from an organization's direct products and services.[33] At The Mighty, a digital media firm, employees circulate and post stories from readers in which readers thank employees for the support, inspiration, or information they have provided. The Mighty's founder begins meetings by asking each employee what their best experience at work was that week; employees radiate pride as they share details about the impact they and others around them had.

My Saint My Hero is a company inspired to transform lives and make the world a better place.[34] Jewelry and wearable blessings sold through the community are fabricated by impoverished women in Bosnia-Herzegovina, Uganda, Italy, and Cambodia; the income these women receive allows them to feed their families, buy shoes for their children, and send them to college. Employees have seen pictures, stories, and films of these women and understand the impact My Saint My Hero has had on their lives. Motley Fool employees are likewise keenly aware of their organization's mission: "Helping the World Invest—Better."[35] In 2015, managers began bringing in clients to thank employees in person and detail how the company has made a difference in their lives. Meanwhile, at the International Monetary Fund (IMF), a minister of finance and benefactors from other countries explained to IMF statisticians and economists how the work they were doing made a difference in their countries. The visitors also offered feedback about what else IMF employees could do to help.

Make Every Moment Count

If you make a practice of giving, specifically in the five ways described in this chapter, you will create a warm, affirming work environment in which civility is the norm. But delivering civility isn't simply about ticking off these items individually; it's about embracing a broader mindset of giving in each and every moment.

Do that, and you'll truly win the hearts and minds of the people around you, generating huge returns for the organization and its stakeholders.

To understand the power of the giving mindset, look no further than Campbell Soup Company. When Doug Conant took over as CEO in 2001, the company had just lost half its market value, sales were declining, and the organization was reeling from a series of layoffs. The environment was so toxic that a Gallup manager described employee engagement as "the worst [he had] ever seen among the Fortune 500."[36]

By 2006, though, Conant had turned things around, and by 2010, employees were setting all-time performance records, outpacing the S&P by a factor of five. Also in 2010, Campbell's was recognized as one of the world's most ethical companies, racking up numerous "bests"—best place to work, best place for women to work, and best place for diversity.[37]

What made the difference? Conant credits two things: being tough-minded on standards and tenderhearted with people.[38] For employees to buy in, they needed to believe that Conant was personally invested in *them*. If he showed that commitment, they in turn would feel committed to the enterprise. Conant put that philosophy to the test on his first day, issuing a pledge to employees that became known as the Campbell Promise: Campbell's will value you.[39]

Conant believed that *how* he showed his personal investment in employees mattered as well. It all came down to employee "touchpoints," or the brief interactions he had daily with employees—in a hallway, in the cafeteria, in a meeting room.[40] If he handled each touchpoint well, he would help employees feel valued and establish himself as a contributor and leader. And Conant didn't just wait for touchpoints to happen; he worked hard to *make* them happen. While CEO, for instance, Conant wrote more than thirty thousand individualized notes of thanks to his twenty thousand employees.[41]

Most of us don't get the opportunity to lead or turn around Fortune 500 companies, but we can still display leadership qualities by giving each and every day. The simple act of congratulating people for a job well done goes a long way toward creating an engaged and productive team. Strive to win the hearts and minds of your people by recognizing, reinforcing, and celebrating their efforts, motivation, and performance. Share success stories. Find ways to highlight progress and a sense of meaning. Donate your time and energy when needed. All of this will inject more civility into your workplace, fueling people and their work.

KEY POINTS

- Share resources, but be smart about it.
- Practice humility and share credit with others who contributed.
- Pay attention to how you give feedback. Identify with the recipient of feedback and understand the emotions he or she is feeling.
- Provide people with a sense of meaningfulness. How is their work positively affecting others?

9

Practice E-civility

The human spirit must prevail over technology.

—Albert Einstein

Ever send an e-mail you wish you could take back? Neal Patterson, CEO of the publicly traded software firm Cerner Corporation, surely has. On March 13, 2001, he decided he didn't like the relatively empty parking lot he found when he arrived at work in the morning at 7:45 a.m. Regarding this as an expression of a company-wide lack of effort, he sent the following electronic message to more than four hundred employees:

> We are getting less than 40 hours of work from a large number of our KC-based EMPLOYEES. The parking lot is sparsely used at 8 a.m.; likewise at 5 p.m. As managers, you either do not know what your EMPLOYEES are doing; or you do not CARE...You have created expectations on the work effort which allowed this to happen inside Cerner, creating a very unhealthy environment. In either case, you have a problem and you will fix it or I will replace you. NEVER in my career have I allowed a team which worked for me to think they

had a 40 hour job. I have allowed YOU to create a culture which is permitting this. NO LONGER....Hell will freeze over before this CEO implements another employee benefit in this culture...I am tabling the promotions until I am convinced that the ones being promoted are the solution, not the problem. If you are the problem, pack your bags...I am giving you two weeks to fix this. My measurement will be the parking lot. It should be substantially full at 7:30 a.m. and 6:30 p.m. The pizza man should show up at 7:30 p.m. to feed the starving teams working late...You have two weeks. Tick-tock.[1]

This entire message was quickly posted to a Yahoo discussion group. The *Wall Street Journal, Financial Times, New York Times, Forbes,* and *Fortune* all ran stories on it. Within three days, Cerner's stock tumbled 22 percent, a loss of roughly $300 million. Patterson's personal wealth plummeted $28 million.

All because of one rude e-mail.

For all the would-be Pattersons out there, here are some quick guidelines for when *not* to send an e-mail:

— You feel the urge to add!!! (to the e-mail)
— You can't resolve a disagreement
— The e-mail will evoke a negative response
— You feel angry
— You feel slighted
— You know the other party is stressed
— You feel stress rising
— The e-mail will deliver bad news

Although e-mail has helped businesses in countless ways, it has also unleashed a torrent of incivility in workplaces. Angry e-mails, e-mails meant to embarrass, inappropriately informal e-mails, excessively long e-mails—the ways a sender can show disrespect are endless, equaled only by the number of ways receivers can show disrespect: by failing to respond on time or at all, by needlessly selecting "reply all," or by forwarding e-mails to make someone look bad. In addition to everything we do to foster civility, we need to get our e-mail etiquette in check so we aren't polite offline and monsters online.

Some Basic Dos and Don'ts

It's easy enough to avoid outbursts like Mr. Patterson's: Focus on being more aware of your emotional state and use some good old-fashioned self-control. It's a bit harder, though, to rein in some of the less dramatic lapses in e-civility. At the root of much of our difficulty with e-mail is the lack of context that exists with this kind of communication. When we write e-mails, our recipients receive only our written words and perhaps an emoticon or two. They don't see our body language and hear our verbal intonations, which convey so much in face-to-face communications. As a result, the potential for misunderstandings and miscues becomes exponentially greater.

The answer is to become far more thoughtful and deliberate about how, when, and why you e-mail. Pay attention to length, thereby respecting your respondents' time. Write with clarity and sincerity. Don't send e-mails indiscriminately. Respond in a timely fashion. Use proper grammar. Don't share private e-mail addresses with a larger group. These and other practices mentioned in the following list are not complicated, but we so often fail to adopt them amidst the rush and tension of our days.[2]

More Rules of E-mail Etiquette

- Write a short but descriptive subject line. Choose utility over creativity.

- Copy people judiciously. Include only those needed.

- Honor e-requests as dependably as requests made face-to-face.

- If you're in doubt about your humor, sarcasm, or criticism, then reread, rethink, and resist the temptation.

- If you're uncertain about your tone, save the message and review it later with a fresh perspective before sending it.

- Consider the time of day you send an e-mail. You can write it now but maybe send it later using delayed delivery.

- Be clear about times, dates, time zones, and any acronyms.

- Before responding to an e-mail, read completely through it.

- Don't mark an e-mail as "urgent" unless it's truly necessary; let the recipient decide for him or herself if it's really "URGENT!!!"

- Avoid using "Notify sender" and follow-up flags.

- Include a signature block with your full name, title, and contact information, especially if the person you're corresponding with has provided this.

- Never send anything to a business e-mail address that the recipient would be embarrassed to have the entire organization read.

- Make sure you put the names in your "To:" field in the proper order, typically by rank or according to the varying degree of responsibility people bear for handling a situation.

- Consider whether an apology is best delivered via e-mail. It might be a great way to start an apology that you later continue in person. If you choose this strategy, include "apology" or "sorry" in the subject line to ensure the recipient opens it.

- Don't select "Reply all" unless absolutely appropriate.
- Don't WRITE MESSAGES IN ALL CAPS.
- Don't forward e-mails to make someone look bad.
- Don't write things in an e-mail that you wouldn't say to a person's face.
- Don't use exclamation points to convey negative emotion. And in serious correspondence, don't use more than one at a time.

Master the Ask

Before you send an e-mail asking for something, make sure it's something you really need and something that's appropriate to request from the receiver.[3] Also, do your part. Don't ask for things that are available online or that you could obtain through more efficient sources.[4] Here are some additional points of etiquette to help you with your e-requests:

- Be brief and direct when making a request. Include who, what, and when.
- If the person needs to act on your message, make that clear in the subject line.
- Thank the recipient—genuinely.
- Don't put the recipient on a tight deadline if possible.
- Don't name times to meet face-to-face or offer small windows of time to talk.
- Give the recipient ample time to respond before following up.

Know When *Not* to Send

How would you feel if you received the following e-mail: "The workforce reduction notification is currently in progress. Unfortunately your position is one that has been eliminated."[5] That's how four hundred RadioShack employees found out that they had lost their jobs. Wholly uncivil. But, sadly, not as rare as it should be. All too often we turn instinctively to e-mail when we're dealing with difficult situations that need to be addressed face-to-face, or at least over the phone. The *number one* act for which people fault themselves in the civility quiz I provided earlier is using e-mail when face-to-face communication is needed. Sensitive issues, conflict situations, and performance reviews all call for an actual, physical presence. A good rule of thumb: If you're wondering whether or not you should send that e-mail, stop. Don't send it. Pick up the phone or meet face to face.

Getting e-mail right isn't about knowing only what not to send but also when not to send—or, for that matter, when not to open. About three-fourths of the thousands of managers and executives I've talked to about e-gadgets find it disrespectful when others use them during meetings. But according to my civility assessment results, nearly 70 percent of people admit to doing so.

John Gilboy, formerly CIO of a multibillion-dollar consumer products company, took a radical approach to uncouth e-mailers. He noticed that his senior team was distracted during their weekly meetings, feverishly typing away on their laptops. Sure, people showed up at meetings, but they were not fully present. It was not only distracting but also dispiriting and stressful.

Desperate to halt such multitasking, Gilboy decided to experiment. At his next meeting, he placed a cardboard box outside the door and required all attendees to drop their smartphones and laptops in so everyone would be fully engaged and attentive. People didn't like this new approach at first, but a few months into it, meetings became so productive that the team was able to cut the length of its meetings in half. What's not to like about that? In addition, people participated more, were more engaged, and had more fun. John's experiment gave his team a taste of what it feels like to be fully present, and they wound up carrying their respectful habits into other meetings and interactions.[6]

Cutting the umbilical cord to laptops and smartphones isn't easy, yet the single biggest complaint I hear from employees about their bosses is that they fail to tune in. Do yourself and others a favor: When you speak or meet with someone, put away your smartphone. Make *others* the priority. You might even go old school and take written notes during conversations. This will signal your desire to remember your employees' points, and they will notice and appreciate the show of respect.

Set a Tone of Respect

Leaders establish norms about respectful e-mail conduct through their own habits and routines. For instance, if leaders typically send out e-mails in the evenings and during the weekends, employees will likely feel compelled to read and respond to them. Even if leaders don't expect responses, their actions tell a different story.

If you write e-mails at all hours, consider placing them in draft folders until working hours or use a delayed delivery service. You'll get a faster reply. According to research based on more than two million e-mail users, people respond to e-mail faster during working hours.[7] Delayed delivery can also be used when you know someone is out of his or her office, on vacation, or in a different time zone. If you're sending e-mails during the workday, don't expect your employees to respond immediately. If you do, you'll find that your employees are distracted, stressed out, and less productive, responding to a deluge of incoming e-mails rather than tackling higher priority items.

When Gloria Mark at the University of California, Irvine, took away e-mail for five days from a group of US Army civilian employees, she found that stress levels, measured by heart monitors, decreased. People reported feeling more in control of their working lives, and they tended to engage in more face-to-face conversations. They also reported being far more productive.[8]

Mark recommends that organizations and leaders encourage employees to read e-mails at limited times during the day versus continually checking for them.[9] Other research has borne out the merits of this approach. In a two-week experiment, researchers asked adults to check their inbox three times a day for a week and another group of adults to check as often as they wanted. The next week, they reversed the instructions for the groups. Employees who checked their e-mail only three times a day reported being far less stressed after one week than employees told to check e-mail freely. The "e-mail-minimalizers" answered roughly as many e-mails as those who checked e-mail often, but in 20 percent less time.[10]

Tackling the Impossible

This chapter has focused on e-mail, but let's step back for a moment and consider the broader online world. According to the *Civility in America 2014* survey, 70 percent of people believe that the Internet encourages uncivil behavior.[11] Yet online incivility is awfully difficult to police. How do we prevent unnerving behavior from trolls? What can we do to better protect people, especially youth, from offensive words and images?

Over the past three years, a team of designers and scientists at Riot Games has partnered with other researchers to tackle this vexing issue, focusing on League of Legends, the most popular PC game, with more than sixty-seven million players worldwide and gross revenues of approximately $1.25 billion.[12] When the Riot

Games team classified online players in terms of their negative and positive behavior, they found that the vast majority of negative behavior—which ranged from trash talk to generally offensive language—didn't stem from habitually toxic online players. Rather, 87 percent of online toxicity originated from players who in general were neutral or positive citizens. Also, the Riot Games team found that pairing a negative player with another negative player created a downward spiral of negative behaviors.[13]

To try to reduce incivility, Riot Games created twenty-four in-game messages or tips to encourage civil behavior such as "Players perform better if you give them constructive feedback after a mistake." Some tips discouraged bad behavior: "Teammates perform worse if you harass them after a mistake." They presented the tips in three colors and at different times during the game. A total of 216 conditions were tested against a control condition, in which no tips were given.[14]

Some tips curbed uncivil behavior. The warning about harassment leading to poor performance reduced verbal abuse by 6.2 percent and offensive language by 11 percent compared with those in the control. This tip had a strong influence only when presented in red, a color associated with error avoidance in Western cultures. A positive message about players' cooperation decreased offensive language by 6.2 percent, and had additional smaller benefits.[15]

The team then implemented cultural reforms within the community of gamers.[16] Given how difficult it is to introduce structure and governance into a society that is anonymous, the team focused on a potent factor: whether or not *consequences* existed for negative and positive behaviors. To deliver meaningful consequences, the team created a mechanism that would allow gamers to offer feedback on behavior in real time. Tribunal, which began in 2011, created public "case files" of behaviors that players themselves had rated as acceptable or unacceptable (players could review game and chat data and vote on each behavior as "acceptable" or "unacceptable"). Each time a player reported another player in Tribunal, the machine learning system was notified; the Riot Games team could then deliver a customized penalty or incentive.[17] The team saw that when players received more specific and immediate feedback, players were more likely to reform their behavior and be civil.[18]

With the Tribunal system in place, the Riot Games team loved what they saw: It turned out that the majority of online gamers/ citizens opposed hate speech. In North America, homophobic slurs were the most rejected phrases.[19]

After some one hundred million Tribunal votes, the Riot Games team began to focus on changing negative words into positive ones. As a result of this initiative, uses of homophobic, sexist, and racist terms have dramatically declined, to the point where they are present in only 2 percent of all League of Legends games. Verbal abuse has plummeted by more than 40 percent. A staggering 91.6 percent of negative players have changed their ways; after being reported for a penalty, they *never* commit another offense. League of Legends is cleaning up its act![20]

Jeffrey "Lyte" Lin, lead game designer of social systems at Riot Games, reported how one boy wrote to him after receiving feedback from peers for using racial slurs. "Dr. Lyte," the boy said, "this is the first time someone told me that you should not use the 'N' word online. I am sorry and I will never say it again."[21]

Riot's research team is experimenting with other ways to improve interactions in this game. They are encouraging sportsmanlike behavior by offering players honor points and other rewards. Riot's team is also studying how to improve language in chat rooms. [22]

We can learn a lot from the efforts of Riot Games: Whether it's during gaming, during our off hours, or during our work-days, we must realize that we can work much more effectively if we practice e-civility. Be more thoughtful about your electronic communications. As with behavior generally, small steps can make a big difference. Practice civility with every e-mail, and you'll gradually make your virtual workplace every bit as pleasant and affirming as your physical one.

KEY POINTS

- Think about how your e-mails might be misinterpreted. If you find yourself doubting your humor, sarcasm, or criticism, then reread, rethink, and resist the temptation.

- Should you even be using e-mail for your message? Or do your emotions, another's emotions, or the issues at hand require a richer form of communication? When in doubt, pick up the phone, set up a conversation via Skype, or meet face-to-face.

- Think about the respectful norms you want to set for sending e-mails. Do you send and expect e-mails at all hours every day?

- Experiment with how often you check e-mail each day. Try to limit yourself to checking and responding three to four times a day. See how it feels and how it affects your productivity.

PART **III**

Lift Your Organization: Cycle to Civility

How can organizations systematically alter their cultures to make them more civil? In part 3, I outline a four-step plan called Cycle to Civility®. The plan covers the entire employee life cycle: recruiting, coaching (orientation and training), scoring (evaluation and rewards), and practicing (improvement, termination, and exit). Although focusing on any of these steps individually will help, you will move your culture toward civility faster if you work on more than one at a time. The more you do, the more apparent it becomes to employees that civility really does run deep.

10

Recruit

There is something more valuable to civilization than wisdom, and that is character.

—H. L. Mencken

Hall of Fame college basketball coach John Wooden once described an extremely productive interview he had with a talented potential recruit. He was at the player's home, and at one point during the conversation, the young man's mother politely asked Wooden a question. Her son then looked at her and snapped, "How can you be so ignorant? Just keep your mouth shut and listen to what Coach says!"[1]

Wooden was shocked. He found the player's behavior completely unacceptable, and it instantly prompted him to reconsider his scholarship offer. "If he couldn't respect her," he reasoned, "how could he possibly respect me when things got tough?" Coach Wooden politely ended the meeting and did not offer the scholarship. The player received other offers and went on to become an extremely successful player with a top program. He even helped defeat Wooden's team, the UCLA Bruins, on more than one occasion. So how could that interview be considered productive? Well, as Wooden said, "[I was] delighted that I had discovered something so important before it was too late, before allowing him to contaminate our team with his 'values.'"[2]

For Wooden, treating others well was paramount: "The important thing," he once noted, "is that you have to care for the others, and not just use them for your own business purposes. And you have to communicate that. If you don't care for them, they will never have that feeling for you, and the organization will suffer when things do turn around."[3] Wooden's culture of civility, like so many others I've seen, began with the way his organization recruited. For Wooden, holding members to high ideals and maintaining exceptional standards of selection was the leader's responsibility, and he had a knack for weeding out trouble before it could contaminate his Bruins—or, as he put it, "keeping a rotting apple out of a barrel of good ones."[4]

To help him in his quest to identify civil players, Wooden designed a character questionnaire that covered many areas of ethical conduct. He used the questionnaire as a guide before he signed a recruit, drawing upon many sources for information about the player: his high school coach and teammates, his pastor, administrators and teachers at his high school, even coaches of opposing teams. Wooden also thoroughly investigated school transcripts and made an effort to check out the recruit's parents and family.[5] For other coaches, a player's skill on the court was the primary—or only—thing to consider. For Wooden, that was just the beginning.

Let Wooden's example inspire you in your own recruiting practices. Don't let germs into your organization. We've examined incivility's general costs, but it's important to register the particular costs that arise when you fail to recruit for civility. As researchers Dylan Minor and Michael Housman found, one toxic employee can wipe out the productivity gains produced by two or more superstars. A superstar (defined as the top 1 percent of workers in terms of productivity) adds about $5,000 to an organization's annual profit, while a toxic worker costs about $12,000 annually.[6] The real difference becomes even greater if other costs are factored in, such as litigation fees, lower employee morale, and dissatisfied customers. My own research on civility shows that rude workers have a stronger negative impact on organizations than civil workers do a positive impact.[7] That's why it's *especially* important to weed out toxic people before they join your organization. And this chapter shows you how.

Interview for Civility

When interviewing potential candidates, use techniques like Wooden's to weed out those who are uncivil. Then throughout the interview process, stay on the lookout for signs of civility. Forgo hypothetical questions, such as "How would you handle...?" or "What would you do if...?" and instead ask the candidate specifically how he or she managed particular situations in the past. Make your organization's values explicit, and inquire how his or her past behavior matches up. Don't just accept the candidate's first answer either; ask for two or three examples.

Use structured interviewing, asking each candidate applying for the job the same questions in the same order. Research shows that these types of interviews more reliably predict a candidate's performance, even with jobs that are unstructured in nature.[8] Consider using the following interview questions:

- What would your former employer say about you—positive and negative?
- What would your former subordinates say about you—positive and negative?
- What about yourself would you like to improve most? How about a second thing? A third?

- What makes you lose your temper? Tell me about the last time this happened.
- Tell me about a time when you've had to deal with stress or conflict at work. What did you do?
- How do you know you're under too much stress? What clues tip you off?
- When have you failed? Describe the circumstances and how you dealt with and learned from the experience.
- What are some examples of your ability to manage and supervise others?
- What kind of people do you find it most difficult to work with? Tell me about a time when you found it difficult to work with someone. How did you handle it?
- What kind of people do you work with best? Tell me about your best team experience.

Also, observe these behaviors:

- Did the candidate arrive promptly for the interview?
- Does the candidate speak negatively of former employers or others?
- Does the candidate take responsibility for behaviors, results, and outcomes, or does he or she prefer to blame others?

It's helpful to register not only what a candidate says but also what they *aren't* saying. When the conversation turns to the specifics that tie to civility, pay attention to possible nonverbal cues. Does the candidate seem visibly pleased to talk about civility, or do you see scowls and fidgeting? How comfortable with your values does the candidate seem?

If your values don't align with the candidate's, it's better to figure that out as soon as possible. Zappos, an online retailer, has prospective customer service representatives attend a ten-day intensive training session in which they learn about the company's culture, strategy, and processes. On the last day of this training, the instructors explain that if the newcomers quit the training session that day, they will be paid for the amount of time they have worked and receive one month's salary (which was up to $3,000 and has since increased).[9]

As part of the interview process, follow up with every employee who encountered the candidate during his or her visit, not just those on the interview schedule. How did the candidate treat your parking lot attendant? Your receptionist? Your administrative assistant? Is the candidate kind, gracious, and respectful or rude and condescending? Many HR professionals have told me that some of the best feedback they receive regarding prospective employees is from the person who drove the candidate from the airport or the receptionist who greeted the candidate at the front desk.

Improve Your Odds

Get your team involved! Have team members go out to lunch or dinner with candidates or take them out to an event, such as a ball game. You want to give candidates a firsthand opportunity to observe your team and organizational values, to help them consider whether they're willing to sign up. If your values don't match, you both can save yourselves a world of time, frustration, and heartache—not to mention save your organization money.

Do Your Homework

A hospital I worked with avoided a near miss when hiring a new radiologist. It offered the job to "Dirk," a talented MD with many solid recommendations. Dirk aced his interviews, but an assistant in the radiology department had a hunch that something was off. Calling her contacts in the field, she learned that Dirk had left many badly treated subordinates in his wake; she reported her findings to the department head. The offer had already gone out, but the department head nixed it, warning Dirk that if he accepted, the hospital would let him go immediately, which could raise a red flag for potential future employers.

Contrast this story with one from another hospital, where a highly talented but uncivil doctor cost his hospital *millions*. Had the hiring committee done its homework, it would have learned about the doctor's history of problem behavior, including formal complaints that had been filed against him at his previous place of employment. Instead, the newly hired MD offended nurses and technicians with his conduct and a lawsuit ensued, taking a steep financial and emotional toll.

It's essential to do your homework on job candidates. As Wooden's example illustrates, properly conducted reference checks can serve as your most valuable tool when selecting employees. Understanding how candidates have behaved in the past will help you assess whether they'll be civil when they come work for you. Ask references for specific behavioral examples of characteristics that get at the heart of civility, such as "What's it like working with Joe?" or "What could Joe improve on?" Share your company's core values with a candidate's references and ask them to describe instances in which the candidate demonstrated those values. Did the candidate's behavior ever reflect negatively upon the organization?

You might also ask

- How did subordinates feel about working for the candidate?
- How emotionally intelligent did the candidate seem? Was he or she able to read people and adjust accordingly?
- Was the candidate comfortable in various situations and working with different types of people?

- How well did the candidate seem to collaborate? Was he or she a team player?
- How did the candidate react to authority?
- Would you rehire this person?

A call, not a letter, is more likely to reveal behavioral problems. Seasoned recruiters report that the most useful data they get from references often comes from follow-up questions, and mainly from the reference's tone, demeanor, and pace, not necessarily their words. Listen closely and follow up on hints of trouble.

Don't just stick to the provided reference list either; talk to your network as well. United States deputy secretary of labor Chris Lu simply picks up the phone and calls people who know the candidate. Chris says it never fails; he gets great information on almost all candidates from his trusted network.

It's also worth talking to a candidate's colleagues from lower levels. Check references with other people who have known the candidate outside work, such as religious leaders, community leaders, professors, or coaches. Plus, take a look at online profiles and social media posts.

How Riot Games Is Using Online Behavior Data

Curious about whether people who are more toxic in games are also more toxic in workplaces, researchers at Riot Games analyzed chat logs from their over 1,800 employees—all of whom played Riot's hugely popular game, League of Legends. Looking at the preceding twelve months of gameplay of every employee, what they found was a high correlation between a player's toxicity and bad behavior in their workplace. Only a small percentage of their workforce (approximately 1.5 percent) showed some form of toxicity in the online game, such as antagonistic game-playing or snarky comments. Yet 25 percent of employees who had been let go in the previous year were players with unusually high toxicity in gameplay. They also took a closer look at Riot's leaders' game behavior, and were pleased to learn that they did not show any signs of toxicity in the online game.[10]

More generally, Riot's researchers found that a player's online toxicity fluctuated. So much so, that they could even measure and predict toxic trajectories. Using these findings, they embarked on improving their employees' player behavior. Riot's leadership took the opportunity to meet with their thirty most toxic employees' (all of whom were more junior Rioters and new to the working world). In each individual meeting, the team brought in-game chat logs to discuss the specific toxic online behavior seen as well as remind them of behavioral expectations. Although these logs factored into the exits of a couple of employees who had already exhibited serious bad behavior, the response from most employees was overwhelmingly positive. "Pretty much everyone we spoke with was appalled at their own behavior. We actually received some essays from employees vowing to change their ways and become not just more considerate gamers but better people," said Jay Moldenhauer-Salazar, Riot's head of Talent.[11]

Riot Games now plans to use job candidates' in-game behavior as an input into their hiring process. They ask applicants for their in-game handle during the application process and review their gameplay to identify uncivil behavior. This information is added to their applicant tracking system where they use a simple stoplight code—red, yellow, green. If the applicant is flagged "red" (the most toxic), a recruiter or hiring manager receives sample (applicant) chat logs to see how an applicant conducts himself in the game he is being considered to work on. By using online behavior data to recruit for civility, and sculpt employee civility, it's no wonder that Riot Games is one of Fortune's 100 best places to work.[12]

Check Your Own Civility

It's hard to expect someone to be civil if you're not modeling the same behavior. John Wooden understood this too. While his many winning seasons garnered respect and admiration, it was his off-the-court behavior and leadership philosophy that elevated him to an American icon, eventually winning him the Presidential Medal of Freedom, among many other accolades. Wooden taught his players that not only believing in values but also *living* them produced poise and confidence that resulted in competitive greatness. "Ability may get you to the top, but character keeps you there," he remarked. So frequently, it's the leader's example that matters the most.[13]

Regardless of what the job is, or how "good" or "bad" a candidate may seem to you, treat him or her respectfully. At Google, internal research shows that candidates' interactions with interviewers are more important to them than the type of work for which they're being considered, the benefits, or their interactions with recruiters.[14] Make sure anyone interviewing candidates is civil in their own right.

I once ran into a star professor, recruited by a university where I worked, who wound up taking a job at one of our rivals. I mentioned that I had really enjoyed his presentation when he was interviewing with us. He immediately launched into what a horrible experience he'd had while interviewing with us because of comments one of our faculty members had made. He said that even though our offer was better in almost every way, including salary and research resources, he feared that this employee reflected our culture—and he wanted no part of it. The most surprising thing of all: The person who had offended him was a junior-level faculty member who would not have been this person's boss or even worked closely with him. Yet that moment of incivility had made all the difference.

Set the standard for civility, and expect everyone you do business with—external advisors, partners, suppliers, and customers—to follow suit. Nike does this: In order to become one of its suppliers, you must sign a letter of agreement in which "respect" is nonnegotiable.

As Nike and Coach Wooden know, skill and talent cannot make up for the damage toxic employees can have on your organization. It's better to catch bad behavior before the person becomes a member of your team. Rely on structured, behavioral interviews. Do your homework. Conduct thorough reference checks. Investigate hunches. And put your own best foot forward. If your initial recruiting efforts don't produce kind, respectful people, don't give up. Keep interviewing until you find people who get it. Amazon.com CEO Jeff Bezos has remarked that he would "rather interview 50 people and not hire anyone than hire the wrong person."[15] Mastering civility takes a little extra effort. But it's worth it.

KEY POINTS

- Interview for civility, using structured interviews with behavioral questions.

- Check references thoroughly, but also go beyond provided references, chasing down leads and hunches.

- Be explicit about your organization's values. Encourage candidates to decide for themselves: Do they truly want to work in an organization where these values reign supreme every day?

11

Coach

Leadership is unlocking people's potential to become better.

—Bill Bradley

Great coaches, like John Wooden, help people understand what to do to perform well, breaking it down into a few manageable steps. They also don't allow players to get too comfortable or forget the basics. Our organizations must do the same when it comes to civility. We must remind people of the fundamentals and help employees stay focused on improving their game. The way organizations can properly coach civility is to set expectations, sculpt civility, create norms, and provide coaching. Let's discuss each in turn.

Set Expectations

You've already articulated your values to prospects during the hiring process. Now that they're with you, make civility a mission for your organization and post it. Coach Wooden didn't stop at recruiting players who lived up to his standards of behavior. Once he had them on the team, he reminded them of his standards using a tool called the Pyramid

of Success, a list of twenty-five character traits that players should inter-
nalize and strive to live by so as to realize their full potential. These
traits included such bedrocks of civility as "cooperation," "friendship,"
"self-control," "team spirit," and "poise." Wooden began each season
handing out copies to student-athletes and plastered the list on his office
wall, expecting his players to live and breathe these traits every day.[1]

Most companies' mission statements contain some language
about how employees should treat customers, but very few mention
anything about how employees should treat one another. However, a
single, simple sentence (e.g., "We expect our employees to treat each
other with respect") can set the tone for civility.

Need some inspiration? Southwest Airlines' mission statement
contains the following: "Above all, employees will be provided the
same concern, respect, and caring attitude within the organization that
they are expected to share externally with every customer."[2] Dignity
Health's list of values includes respect for the inherent worth of each
person, collaboration, justice (including advocating for social change
and acting in ways that promote respect for all persons and demonstrate
compassion for those who are powerless), and stewardship (cultivating
the resources entrusted to us to promote healing and wholeness).[3]

Starbucks' mission statement, "To inspire and nurture the
human spirit—one person, one cup, and one neighborhood at a
time,"[4] appears strongly consistent with civility, and the company's
values make this explicit in outlining how employees are expected to
treat one another. The company's values include "Creating a culture
of warmth and belonging, where everyone is welcome" and "Being
present, connecting with transparency, dignity, and respect."[5]

Beyond mission or vision statements, organizations should clearly
explain their basic code of conduct to employees. They might follow
the example of another successful coach from the world of sports, the
NFL's Pete Carroll. Early in his career as a college football coach, Carroll found great success—including national championships and two

Coach of the Year Awards—through a positive, supportive coaching style. Moving to the Seattle Seahawks, Carroll "wanted to find out if we went to the NFL and really took care of guys, really cared about each and every individual, what would happen."[6] Carroll's approach required that everyone employed by his team—coaches, players, personal assistants, and valets—behave in a thoughtful, positive way toward others. Civility replaced the usual yelling and swearing that took place in locker rooms and on the sidelines. Seahawk players and coaches closed every media interview by thanking the reporter. The physical and mental well-being of *everyone* mattered.[7]

And Carroll didn't communicate his approach in an abstract way; he boiled it down to three rules that will go far toward engendering mutual respect in any organization:

1. Protect the team.
2. No whining, no complaining, no excuses.
3. Be early.[8]

The goal? Signal how much you value each player. Respect one another and the organization.

Did Carroll's clearly articulated norms of civility enable the Seahawks to win games? That's impossible to say. One thing, though, is certain: It didn't hurt. In Carroll's fourth year as head coach, the Seahawks won the Super Bowl.

Sculpt Civility

Reinforce civility at every turn. Make it second nature—so familiar that people don't even think about it; they just do it. Emphasize civility's importance during employee orientations. Repeat it like a mantra. Make it a talking point at every meeting. Challenge employees to master civility fundamentals.

One company that "sculpts" civility well is Chick-fil-A.[9] In an interview with me, president and chief operating officer Tim Tassopoulos noted that customers are "wowed by civility" at the company's independently operated restaurants and impressed by Chick-fil-A's efforts to deliver it. Chick-fil-A owner-operators encourage their employees—including many teenagers working their first jobs—to go the extra mile for customers, pulling out chairs for patrons and carrying meals to their tables for them.[10] Chick-fil-A franchisees place special emphasis on polite and pleasant language; employees are expected to say "It's my pleasure" and to ask "May I refresh your beverage?" instead of "Can I refill your drink?"

Notwithstanding its imperfections (keep in mind, no company is perfect), how does Chick-fil-A inspire its young team members to be so civil so consistently? According to Tassopoulos, the brand's culture is built on servant leadership, as embodied in its SERVE model: *See* and shape the future, *Engage* and develop others, *Reinvent* continuously, *Value* results and relationships, and *Embody* the company values. Tassopoulos attributes about 80 percent of the firm's success with culture to selection around these values and communicating them during the selection process. The company carefully chooses independent operators who enjoy serving others and love building a culture devoted to service. The remaining 20 percent is owed to the company's efforts to sculpt civility by reinforcing it.

At individual stores, Chick-fil-A owner-operators coach employees on its values during employee orientation and training. Customers then provide feedback on how employees are delivering on those values, and individual operators (franchisees) access that data and use it to coach team members.

Tassopoulos notes that sculpting civility is much more effective if leaders are living the values themselves. Individual operators often live the values, and when they do, the company makes a point of telling others about it. In January 2014, a severe snowstorm unexpectedly pummeled the southern United States, stranding thousands of motorists. A Chick-fil-A operator in Birmingham, Alabama, and his team members decided to take food to these motorists; many team members who had been sent home early returned to lend a hand. The operator also opened up the restaurant to those in need of shelter. An employee explained, "This company is based on taking care of people and loving people before you're worried about money or profit. . . . We were just trying to follow the model that we've all worked under for so long and the model we've come to love. There was really nothing else we could have done but try to help people any way we could."[11]

In January 2015, that same store was featured in the media. This time, the operator was caught on video giving a meal to a needy man who had asked to work for food. But it didn't stop there. The operator retrieved his own gloves and gave them to the man since it was very cold. A mother in the store watching the incident went up to the operator in tears and told him how moved she was. She thanked him, explaining how much she appreciated his actions as a teaching moment for her son, who was sitting with her. It didn't take long before she posted the incident and it went viral.[12]

Yet another teaching moment for Chick-fil-A occurred in December 2015, when a restaurant in Rockwall, Texas, seemingly broke with the company's policy of staying closed on Sundays. Employees opened the store to serve food to first responders and people whose homes had been destroyed by a deadly tornado that had hit the day before.[13] Operators and their employees company-wide learned about their colleagues' efforts on behalf of the local community—a great opportunity for the company to sculpt civility by illustrating that being closed for business doesn't mean you aren't able to serve your community in a time of crisis.

Thanks in part to its ongoing efforts to reinforce civility, Chick-fil-A has seen sales rise by about 10 percent almost every year of its existence. In 2015, the company earned the number two spot (behind Amazon.com) in *USA Today*'s Customer Service Hall of Fame and took the top spot for restaurants and sixth overall in Prophet's 2016 Brand Relevance Index. The company also was listed in the top 10 of 24/7 Wall St.'s 2015 America's Best Companies to Work For, among other honors.[14]

Find creative ways to encourage and reinforce civility. During a yearlong civility campaign at the National Security Agency, leaders engaged employees in a thoughtful dialogue on the importance of civility, bringing in speakers, creating a civility "Wall of Fame" honoring civil employees, devoting part of their website to articles written by employees on what civility means to them, and planting "challenge cards" all over their office. The last of these was especially successful. Employees received business-sized cards with a personal civility challenge that began with "Civility starts with you..." Challenges were as basic as "Hold the door open for at least five people this week" or "This week, resist the urge to point out others' mistakes." Such challenges brought civility alive for employees, making them aware of and focusing them on specific behaviors. Employees appreciated the challenges and had fun with them. The office became even more civil.

Create Norms

Don't simply impose civility. Engage employees in an ongoing conversation, defining precisely what civility means. You will garner more support and empower employees to hold one another accountable for civil behavior by involving them in the process.

From his first meeting with the 2008 US men's Olympic basketball team, Coach K (Mike Krzyzewski, coach at Duke University) set two clear standards for his players' conduct: (1) look one another in the eye, and (2) always tell the truth. He also asked each team member to contribute his own ideas, promising that any idea agreed upon by all players would be added to the team's standards. The team produced fifteen guidelines that everyone agreed to, including

Jason Kidd's suggestion: "We shouldn't be late and we should respect one another." After the team won gold, Coach K explained, "We never had a guy late and we never had a bad practice. . . . It was me asking them, 'What do you guys believe in?' "[15]

Organizations of all kinds can benefit from talking about civility with employees. In the Irvine, California, office of law firm Bryan Cave, managing partner Stuart Price and I led employees through an exercise in which they could define collective norms. We asked employees the pivotal question I described at the outset of this book: "Who do you want to be?" And we asked them to name rules for which they were willing to hold one another accountable—what norms were right for their organization. In just over an hour, employees generated and agreed upon ten norms. The firm embraced these norms and bound them into a "civility code," which they prominently display in their lobby. As Price attests, the civility code was directly responsible for the firm being ranked number one among Orange County's Best Places to Work.[16]

Bryan Cave's Code of Civility

1. We greet and acknowledge each other.

2. We say please and thank you.

3. We treat each other equally and with respect, no matter the conditions.

4. We acknowledge the impact of our behavior on others.

5. We welcome feedback from each other.

6. We are approachable.

7. We are direct, sensitive, and honest.

8. We acknowledge the contributions of others.

9. We respect each other's time commitments.

10. We address incivility.

It's not enough to frame norms; you also have to train employees to understand and respect them. When asked why they were uncivil, more than 25 percent of people in one survey blamed their organization for not providing them with the basic skills they needed, such as listening and feedback skills.[17] If your employees aren't behaving well, and you've already gone through the trouble of hammering home the organization's civility message, ask yourself, "Have I also equipped them to succeed?" Don't assume everyone instinctively knows how to be civil; many people never learned the basic skills.

To teach employees these skills, you might create a workshop module on workplace civility that covers what civility looks like, describes situations in which employees sometimes act uncivilly, provides tips on how to maintain composure, and affords opportunities to practice behaving civilly in emotionally charged situations. Some leading-edge companies are already offering formal civility training. Microsoft's popular Precision Questioning class teaches participants to question their own ideas; develop approaches to healthy, constructive criticism; and act with emotional agility even in tense situations. At a hospital in Los Angeles, temperamental doctors are required to attend "charm school" to decrease their brashness and reduce the potential for lawsuits. The "charm school" teaches doctors that they must set the tone for their medical residents.

This hospital also trains its employees to watch out for unreported instances of incivility, such as staff members refusing to work with particular doctors, complaints about nurses circulating through the grapevine, and residents seeming to steer clear of certain "mentors." As the hospital previously realized, nurses, staff, and residents often failed to report bad behavior formally. They kept their complaints to themselves until they were pushed too far and felt compelled to file a lawsuit. Since doctors were the ones dealing with these folks on a daily basis (and HR was relatively removed from the situation), doctors needed to stay alert to the warning signs. At this hospital, doctors were both empowered and *required* to report all incidents. If they neglected this responsibility, the hospital held them personally responsible for the consequences. The hospital did a great job of creating norms and embedding them firmly within the culture.

Provide Coaching

Beyond formal training, coach employees on specific civility fundamentals to get your employees in tip-top form. Help them to listen fully, give and receive feedback (positive and corrective), work across differences, and deal with difficult people. You might also coach them on negotiation, stress management, crucial conversations, and mindfulness. The following outlines some tips to guide you in the coaching process.

Don't just impart information. A coach who reviews fundamental concepts and expectations must also be ready to hold his or her employees accountable, pointing out bad behavior for first-time offenders. Some Chick-fil-A franchise operators evaluate team members weekly using red, yellow, and green lights.[18] The idea is to quickly catch and correct anything needed. Zingerman's has huddles where a team will review how they're doing and make adjustments. They'll track how long it's taking for customers to be properly greeted, for example.[19]

When offering personal coaching to individual employees, try using upward evaluations or 360 feedback (anonymously collected and consolidated across respondents). In-person, peer-to-peer coaching is another option; here you'll want to focus on the basics, having peers ask one another "What do you like about what I'm doing, and what do you *not* like about what I'm doing?"

One organization found that employees did not always want to formally escalate a problem, and in some cases, weren't comfortable raising the issue with their manager or HR team. They created a peer-to-peer advisor network that provides an opportunity for employees to discuss situations and concerns in as confidential a setting as possible. Advisors are local peers who understand local culture, environment, and laws. Advisors are trained to help employees explore options to address their issue. They are not case managers and are not intended to escalate cases on behalf of the employee, rather serve as empathetic listeners to help empower them to make a decision about how to move forward.

As I mentioned in chapter 5, when I work with MBAs and executives, I have them offer one another feedback using a "Who's in Your Group?" exercise, in which they indicate who in the group demonstrates particular positive or negative behaviors (please see my chart of this in the Actions and Impact for Your Group and Organization section). I also have teammates complete an index card for each member, providing specific suggestions for how that person might wield greater influence. On one side of the card, participants provide information on strengths. On the other side of the card, each member identifies three things this teammate should work on to become more influential. I tell MBAs and executives to be very specific with one another about nonverbals, tics, and habits that may limit their potential.

Becoming a more civil team or organization requires that you set expectations clearly and then enforce civility through constant repetition. But don't stop there. Be sure to define the specific behaviors your organization is seeking, engaging your team in a discussion about who they want to be and what norms they are willing to live by. Teammates can greatly help one another live up to organizational standards, politely calling each other out when someone deviates from organizational norms. To top it off, the organization can provide coaching of various kinds to help both those struggling with the fundamentals and those who have trouble living by the norms.

KEY POINTS

- Make civility part of your mission statement, posting it somewhere visible so employees are reminded daily of your organization's standards.

- Engage your team in a dialogue about what your norms should be. Then ask them to hold one another accountable.

- Train or coach employees, paying attention to how you offer feedback.

- Employ coaches for anyone who is failing to live up to your standards.

12

Score

A crucial measure of our success in life is the way we treat
one another every day of our lives.

—P. M. Forni

What if you had a way to rate an e-mail a colleague sent you, or a status
update a friend posted on social media, solely based on how respectful
it sounded? That would be a game changer, wouldn't it? One concept
would be simple: Use an online tool to provide instant feedback about
the civility of a person's communications—similar to Facebook's emoji
or thumbs-up feature; the person could learn how they are perceived
and moderate their behavior accordingly. I don't know of organizations
that are scoring civility systematically. Although many organizations
now hire for civility and emphasize civility, respect, inclusion, and dignity in their mission statements, they're not measuring it. A few companies have unrolled metrics like "interpersonal skills," "emotional
competency," or "being a team player."[1] Years ago, Microsoft began
including "emotional competence" in all employee performance evaluations. Several of Google's eight Project Oxygen attributes—used to rate
managers—reflect civility: "Express interest/concern for team members'

success and personal well-being," "Be a good communicator—listen and share information," and even "Be a good coach."[2] But in most organizations, traditional metrics and focus win out.

If you value civility (and I'm hoping you do now!), then you should show how much it matters to you and your organization. And the best, most compelling way to send that message is to recognize and reward civility. Coach Wooden was careful to measure and reward values he cared about, including kindness and respect toward others. In basketball, the metric that typically attracts the most attention is "points scored." But in Wooden's eyes, the team as a whole is what mattered most, not individual stars, so he created a system that emphasized the individual's contributions to the team.

Wooden insisted that the post-season awards for his team go not only to the top-scoring athletes but also to the players who exemplified qualities tied to his pyramid of values—qualities like improvement, attitude, contributions to the team, and other acts that strengthened the organization as a whole. On an informal basis, he was careful to single out individuals who seldom saw the limelight—the players who made an assist on an important basket, a pivotal defensive play, or a free throw at a crucial point in the game. Wooden also monitored and recognized those who didn't get much playing time—the players who worked hard to improve and who pushed their teammates to improve as well.[3]

What's your current system of performance metrics like? Does it help foster the civil behaviors you're trying to encourage? Are you promoting behaviors like giving or collaborating well with others? If not, then this chapter suggests a few key things you can do to start.

Go Beyond Results

First, focus more generally on the *how* of work when evaluating performance and not just the actual results. When founding W. L.

Gore and Associates, Bill Gore wanted to create a company without traditional hierarchy and titles, an organization where everyone spoke to everyone, and every employee contributed to designing innovative products.[4] He wanted his company to retain its familial, collegial feel as it grew. Bill Gore managed to accomplish these goals while achieving remarkable business success in part because of the company's performance management system, which focuses not merely on what people are contributing but also on *how* they're living the company's values.[5]

W. L. Gore's values are clearly defined, and people are expected to "walk the talk" every day. A glance at its leadership effectiveness survey reveals that Gore's leaders are evaluated against many metrics that bear some relation to civility, including

- "encourages collaboration and networking across the enterprise";
- "creates an environment of trust with associates";
- "encourages diversity of thought and perspective in decision making";
- "trusts and empowers teams and individuals to make decisions, as appropriate"; and
- "invests sufficient time in making the culture work effectively."[6]

Each Gore leader and associate is typically evaluated by twenty to thirty peers and, in turn, evaluates twenty to thirty peers. A cross-functional committee of leaders discusses the results and develops an overall ranking of the company.[7] "No system is perfect," CEO Terri Kelly explains, "but ours levels the playing field and allows real talent to emerge and get compensated accordingly.... If you focus on values and fundamentals, that's how you drive values."[8]

Critically, the peer evaluations focus on results as well as the manner in which people work. How might your company measure the *how* of work? Think about the type of work that gets done and the way kindness and respect might come into play. Use that to arrive at a formulation of appropriate evaluation metrics. Then combine these metrics with more conventional metrics that measure performance.

Thank People for Helping

We've seen that expressing gratitude is an important dimension of civility, yet all too often we fail to register the full contributions people make, and thus we fail to bestow upon them the gratitude they deserve. We need to adjust our performance metrics to account for what people are actually doing to push the organization forward.

For instance, the time employees spend engaged in "collaborative" work—attending meetings, making phone calls, answering e-mails—has increased in recent decades by about 50 percent, now constituting 80 percent or more of employees' time.[9] Yet most performance management systems aren't capturing *how* employees interact with one another—the very basics of effective collaboration. As we've seen, a large proportion of value-added contributions wind up originating from only 3 to 5 percent of employees.[10] A study led by Ning Li of the University of Iowa showed how a single "extra miler," who helps colleagues beyond what his or her role requires, can drive performance more than all the other teammates combined.[11]

Most organizations don't recognize such all-star helpers for their contributions: Research has shown that only 50 percent of the top collaborative contributors are deemed to be "top performers" and roughly 20 percent of organizational stars don't help others very much.[12] They may hit their numbers and reap the lion's share of the awards, but they fail to contribute to or amplify the success of their colleagues.

True top performers often suffer from burnout as a result of the overwhelming demands placed on them.[13] In data on business unit line leaders across twenty organizations, researchers found that the highest collaborators turned out to have the lowest engagement and career satisfaction scores. Ultimately, these valuable collaborators left their organizations, taking knowledge and network resources along with them. Or they stayed but spread their growing apathy or frustration to other colleagues.[14]

A simple thank you would go a long way toward helping all-star collaborators stay engaged. It's hardly civil to essentially ignore the people on your team who are helping far more than their peers. They deserve our thanks, and they deserve to be recognized as top performers in the organization. Ask yourself, "What am I doing to measure collaboration, identify top performers, and thank them for their efforts?"

Mobilize Networks to Track Civility

Social network analysis is a wonderful tool that can help us determine the nuances of relationships: How are people perceived? How valuable are they? How are they scored for civility?[15] Such analysis also allows us to comprehend the bigger picture: How is a team playing? Who is working well with others, helping them to notch wins? Who is bringing departments together or keeping them apart? Who is energizing others or bringing them down? And how are these relationships affecting the team, the network, the organization?

My colleagues and I studied in an engineering firm the effects of de-energizing relationships—relationships in which one person possesses an enduring, recurring set of negative judgments, feelings, and behavioral intentions toward another person. We found that employees who perceived more people as de-energizing were twice as likely to voluntarily leave the organization. Unfortunately for this firm, high performers with an above-average number of de-energizing ties were *thirteen times* more likely to leave than low and average performers with the same number of de-energizing ties.[16]

To prevent these and other losses, it's crucial to identify uncivil and de-energizing ties. Managers might sense a problem between two individuals, but it's much harder to detect broader issues (such as an incivility bug). Organizational or social network analysis brings these underlying issues to the fore. We use short, ten-minute surveys to ascertain the positive or negative health of groups of employees. We ask employees to evaluate their positive and negative relationships with others as well as the perceived civility of their fellow employees. We combine this data to create network maps and measures. This data then allows us to evaluate individual relationships as well as how civility or incivility is affecting the network as a whole.[17]

Social network analysis also helps to identify whether a person is primarily the source or the recipient of civility, incivility, and de-energizing relationships. We've found that de-energizing behavior usually stems from stress rather than a single individual's personality.[18] This information has prompted managers to make adjustments (to workload, for example) and to provide helpful resources and support.

Sometimes network analysis reveals larger issues within an organization. Informal organizational networks tend to consist of hubs of highly connected people, and only a small number of ties connect the hubs together. If the connections between different network hubs consist of de-energizing people (e.g., an uncivil colleague), then little interaction will exist between the groups. In one instance, we found that the only tie between a branch of an oil and gas organization in Africa and its sister branch in Europe was de-energizing. Because of the negative nature of this one relationship linking the two groups, little dialogue or exchange of ideas took place. Network analysis brought this issue to the manager's attention and led him to promote greater interaction between others in the two units. Problem solved.[19]

Network studies also help to shine a light on your most civil, valuable employees. You may find hidden gems that connect teams or departments in your organization, allowing for information exchange and enhanced collaboration. If you've been overlooking these individuals, they're going underappreciated and unrewarded. Thank them for helping make your organization a more civil place!

Measure Down and Across, Not Just Up

To measure civility well, take a page from W. L. Gore's playbook and gather scoring input from all levels. When it comes to incivility, people tend to kiss up and kick down; you thus need to understand what subordinates *and* peers *and* bosses think of an employee. The 360 feedback many organizations currently utilize can work great, but only if sufficient trust exists. If employees don't feel confident about the anonymity of their input and how it's being used, their 360 feedback will misinform you.

Google's Manager Feedback Survey (MFS) allows teams to give confidential feedback on their managers, including how much consideration he or she shows toward the employee.[20] Managers who score low on individual items receive a nudge to seek help or instruction in that particular area. Google also encourages managers to share their results with employees and discuss how they might improve their performance; coaching and specific recommendations from employees guide improvement.

When it comes to recognizing civil conduct, peer assessments are also often underutilized. It's a shame since peers are the employees most likely to recognize positive behavior when it happens. Mindful of this reality, some companies are going so far as to mobilize peers to reward acts of kindness or respect. Google's gThanks is a tool that makes it easy to send thank-you notes; all an employee has to do is enter a colleague's name, hit a button marked "kudos," and type a note.[21] Delivered kudos are posted publicly and can be shared. After the launch of gThanks, Google found the use of kudos increased 460 percent as compared with a previous kudos website Google had used.[22]

Any Zappos employee who sees a coworker doing something special can award a "Wow," which includes cash rewards of up to fifty dollars. All recipients of a "Wow" are automatically eligible for Zappos' coveted Hero awards, which are selected by top executives. Those chosen receive a covered Hero parking spot for a month, a one-hundred-fifty-dollar Zappos gift card, and, not least, a hero's cape!

Motley Fool implemented a new peer-to-peer employee recognition program, YouEarnedIt,[23] which enables Fools to reward their coworkers with "gold" for any action they feel worthy: helping with projects, hitting a major deadline, or mentoring. Employees can redeem the gold for gift cards and merchandise. The YouEarnedIt's live feed allows employees to read all posted compliments. It's a way to share information and celebrate accomplishments related to both results and the *how* of work. Each month, a small group of recognized Fools are selected to attend a special off-site event, such as a soccer match or concert. This brings together different Fools, further building camaraderie and team spirit.

If you want to build a civil organization, make sure you're evaluating it. People can get cynical quickly if you say civil behavior is important but you fail to keep track of it. Scoring civility communicates how strongly you value it. Orient yourself to measuring the *how* of work. Thank the often-invisible helpers in your organization. Mobilize social network analysis to uncover both civility and rudeness. Enlist peers and subordinates to monitor, reward, and thank the people who behave well. Measuring civility may not be conventional, but, as we've seen, civil cultures are—sadly—not conventional either. Take your metrics to the next level by using them to capture respect and kindness.

KEY POINTS

- Align your evaluation system to your organization's values. Make sure you're motivating and reinforcing behaviors that help you achieve organizational goals.

- Recognize and reinforce actions that lead to results for the organization. Who do you depend on to help your team score your goals? Recognize the people who dole out assists.

- Create a culture in which employees are credited for the how. Encourage people to appreciate the acts that set them up for success.

CHAPTER **13**

Practice

Nothing will work unless you do.

—John Wooden

What do you do if your evaluation or scoring system uncovers employees who are behaving uncivilly? You have two options: work with them or show them the door. Most companies I consult with decide to expend at least some effort working with offenders—and rightfully so. Only 4 percent of people I surveyed claim they're uncivil because it's fun and they can get away with it. That means the vast majority of employees who behave rudely can improve their behavior. As one CEO put it, they can be "recycled." Of course, some employees are more recyclable than others. A top executive leading the people of a high-technology Fortune 500 company told me that employees "have to be willing to see it and hear [feedback]. They have to be willing to work at it and not just put it in the drawer."

Let's start with the assumption that it's worth it for a company to "recycle" people who are spreading around the nasty incivility bug, recasting them into productive contributors. And let's also assume that most of your employees are both willing and able to receive feedback and do something with it. Under these conditions, your organization should help employees by providing corrective feedback and giving them a chance to practice new behaviors. As Coach Wooden stressed, "It's the little details that are vital. Little things make big things happen."[1] To get the details right, you must show courage as a leader, correcting bad behavior quickly and firmly while also educating employees on what they should do to change. Let's take a few minutes to see how you might best work with an employee who has behaved uncivilly. We'll also examine how to handle an employee's exit if the opportunity to practice doesn't bear fruit.

Establish a Feedback Loop

To help change people's behavior, I recommend following a specific feedback loop described by coaching guru Marshall Goldsmith. This loop comprises four steps: evidence, relevance, consequence, and action.[2] *Evidence* should have been revealed during the evaluation stage; for instance, a manager receives feedback that he doesn't listen to employees or he tends to demean employees in front of others.

To establish the *relevance* of this feedback, ask yourself how the manager compares with his peers. Is his performance suffering because of his subpar, uncivil behavior? If so, the feedback becomes relevant.

You should attach *consequences* to the uncivil behavior so as to motivate change. As Goldsmith has remarked, "People will do something—including changing their behavior—only if it can be demonstrated that doing so is in their own best interests as defined by their own values."[3] Since we tend to respond more strongly to potential losses versus potential gains,[4] it's important to show offenders what they stand to lose if they don't improve. For most people, the potential loss of a promised promotion is strong motivation to behave more civilly.

If you're satisfied that the employee wants to improve, it's time to proceed to the *action* phase. First, develop a plan with the employee. What do you want him to achieve? What will make him more effective? What do you expect him to change? How will he achieve these plans? Strive for clearly defined, tangible, trackable goals. From here, start the hard work of practicing. Working alone or with the assistance of a coach or mentor, the employee should identify the trigger(s) of his bad behavior. What circumstances or people provoke him? Since the key to civility is self-awareness, it's best if the employee answers this question for himself, understanding his actions and connecting them to an underlying cause, such as stress or a feeling of insecurity.

After an employee has identified the triggers and understands the consequences, Goldsmith has them apologize—ideally face-to-face—to everyone affected by their uncivil behavior and ask them for help in getting better. The employee shouldn't explain, complicate, or qualify the behavior, because doing so risks diluting the message.[5] Goldsmith also advises helping the employee to advertise their efforts so that people know he or she is trying to change. Think back to the executive in chapter 5 who enlisted her team to help her stop interrupting people in meetings and commandeering their ideas. This executive let her team know about it and then was able to follow up with them at various points to gauge her improvement.

Following up is especially important.[6] Goldsmith's research reveals that people don't improve if they don't follow up.[7] An employee who checks in with colleagues every month for twelve to eighteen months reminds the colleagues that he or she is trying and values their opinion. It allows colleagues to erase their skepticism about the person's ability to change, and it serves as an open acknowledgment that change will be an ongoing process.[8] Following up also gives the employee a sense of progress, which increases both engagement and motivation.[9]

Most organizations that "recycle" offenders do so by calling upon others to help offenders hone their skills. Companies often encourage offending personnel to share their development objectives with key stakeholders, including managers, teammates, and direct reports. These stakeholders become involved in the employee's growth by becoming aware of the objectives and offering future-focused objectives that tie to these areas of development. Several Fortune 100 companies strongly encourage managers who behave uncivilly to share all evaluations with their team so that team members can provide specific suggestions for improvement. Managers are nudged to engage in "feedforward" to elicit useful ideas for the future on how to improve behavior.

Can You Really Cure Incivility?

You might wonder whether Goldsmith's feedback loop actually succeeds. Goldsmith's data on eighty-six thousand participants suggests that it often does.[10] It's true that not everyone responds to a feedback loop, at least not in the way their organizations desire. Although nearly 100 percent of Goldsmith's participants claimed they were going to act on lessons learned, only 70 percent did; 30 percent did nothing. This 70/30 split held across all eight organizations Goldsmith studied. When he looked at the 70 percent who had taken action, he found that the people who improved followed up with others. They also tackled improvement as a process that unfolded over time and with practice.

In my work with companies, I've seen a Goldsmith-style feedback loop make a huge difference. At one consulting firm, a partner with a perfectionist ethic had gotten into the habit of blasting people for perceived failures in their work. A coach worked with him to identify his triggers, which turned out to involve insecurity and an aversion to vulnerability. The coach helped him understand the potential consequences of his continued incivility. People had become fearful of him; they didn't speak up or share ideas because they feared he would publicly and harshly tear them down. Many dreaded working with him, and some had already left. If this partner didn't improve, his business results would decline, and in short order his fellow partners would likely push him out.

The partner recognized the damage he was doing and apologized to his employees. He let them know that he was working on his perfectionist ways and that he was determined to treat them better. Within a few short months, he became far more mindful of his destructive habits. When he wanted to lash out or admonish people, he caught himself and reminded himself of the impact. This partner also made a point of letting his employees know that he valued the work they did. Sometimes he slipped and treated an employee poorly; in these cases, he went back and apologized. Every month, he checked in with employees to gauge how they were viewing his progress. Hearing how much it meant to employees that he valued them reinforced his efforts and his commitment to improve.

It's important for consequences to be clear and meaningful. Some partners at a law firm decided to change only after being threatened with a loss of equity shares. Once the organization linked uncivil behavior to their pocketbooks, they finally improved their civility. As a coach or a manager looking to motivate a change in behavior, you need to look for that hot button. What is it that might flip the switch and get someone to be more civil? Is it money? A reduction in status or power? Or simply the knowledge that continued rudeness will compromise the offender's popularity with his or her peers? Whatever that hot button is, find it and press on it in the service of civility.

Don't Compromise on Incivility

Sometimes, despite considerable effort, you can't get through to an employee and convince them to make the effort. In that case, stay strong and don't compromise, even if you risk losing a talented or seemingly valuable employee. In one Fortune 500 organization, a brilliant engineer who had risen through the ranks was having problems working well with others. His managers tried the bubble approach, isolating him and keeping him away from other people. However, since his engineering work required collaborating with others, that approach didn't work very well. The organization hired a coach to work with him, but he just didn't seem to care. An employee explained to me that "it was tough to imagine that [this offender] could be so oblivious and callous." At one point, while working in Latin America, the engineer made fun of the clients' accents. That was it, the last straw. The organization fired him.

Danny Meyer, owner of twenty-seven restaurants in New York City, preaches civility and tolerates nothing less.[11] If bad behavior from an employee at any level isn't corrected quickly, they're gone. Meyer is convinced that customers can taste incivility. Even exceptional chefs don't last in Meyer's restaurants if they're disrespectful to other employees.

Taking a hard line is smart, because if you don't deal with incivility, you're opening yourself up to any number of unpleasant consequences. When employees are treated badly by their coworkers, 80 percent will tell others inside and outside the organization. About one-fourth will project their unhappiness onto customers and decrease their assistance to coworkers. Meanwhile, chronic offenders will continue their bad behavior, feeling ever more certain that they're "safe." This behavior will spread, with colleagues and subordinates assuming that (a) bad behavior is acceptable to you, (b) the offender is more powerful than you are, or (c) both.

A former entertainment executive, whom I'll call Zarger, described his encounters with a high-profile director-producer who, during the filming of a big movie, "strolled through a warehouse full of extras, publicly admonishing crew members." Zarger added,

"It didn't take long before the third assistant director learned from the diatribe and mimicked the behavior on the layer below him." Soon, even lower-level crew members openly referred to the extras as "nothing but props that eat."

You might think that moving chronic offenders to other areas of the company will solve the problem. Don't fool yourself. Once moved, offending employees will resume their bad behaviors and infest other parts of your organization. More managers and executives these days are growing wary of such reassignments. A few have told me that they won't even consider hiring internally anymore because they've been burned by the handoff.

Don't just stand tough when it comes to uncivil employees; apply the same strict standards of behavior to customers, suppliers, and other stakeholders. Remember Southwest Airlines' credo that employees must grant each other the "same respect and caring attitude" they give customers? Well, what if a customer treats a SWA employee uncivilly? Southwest still means business. My favorite example is the SWA manager who escorted a belligerent passenger to another airline's counter, where she bought him a ticket to fly the competitor![12]

Leaders and managers love to make excuses for why they shouldn't deal strictly with an uncivil person. They say "He doesn't really mean any harm" or "It's easier to keep him than to find a replacement." They say "We can't afford to lose her," "This is just who he is," or "She's not so bad, really." Do yourself and your organization a favor and lose the excuses. Get real about uncivil conduct. Stay tough.

Some decades ago, a Jewish student left the University of Notre Dame because he was repeatedly hazed by his dormmates. The president of the university summoned the perpetrators and delivered this directive: "Pack your bags. Go find your friend. Either you persuade him to come back to Notre Dame or you don't come back."[13] Now, that's tough. And when it comes to rudeness in the workplace, it's equally appropriate.

Handling the Exit

When you show offending employees the door, be sure to treat these people well on their way out, and while you're at it, take another look at your termination procedures with civility in mind. When employees leave your organization, no matter what the reasons, do you treat them respectfully? Employees who remain, even those who favor the exit, are watching. They're imagining that someday they could be treated the same way.

How you treat people—especially during difficult times—can make or break relationships and networks, including those that will influence your future. The world continues to grow more connected. A lot of damage can be done via social media. Think *Who do I want to be?* and take the high road. Try to end on the best terms possible.

An executive I know well was leading a charity event, and he posted information on LinkedIn. Later, he learned that a former employee had seen the posting and made a very generous contribution. This employee had been fired—civilly. If you doubt whether that made any difference, compare this situation with the general manager in chapter 1 who sat with his feet propped up on the table.

Follow up after people leave your organization. During exit interviews, ask employees how they were treated while working for your organization. Listen very carefully. Most employees are reluctant to burn bridges, but some will tell you what has happened if they think you really care. About six months after an employee has left, conduct a post-departure interview. By then, the former employee will have established him- or herself in a new job and may share additional insights with you.

If your industry is too small or if the offender is too powerful, targets of incivility might fear that coming forward will ruin their careers. I still contend that post-departure interviews hold promise. They're relatively inexpensive and they do pay off. Sometimes the new environment gives targets clearer insight into their former experiences with incivility, and that makes them ready to share those insights. It's worth a shot.

I've laid out a comprehensive, four-part approach for building more civil cultures in organizations. As you've seen, if you get recruiting, coaching, scoring, and practicing right, you'll win. By recruiting well, you save yourself and your organization time and money. You prevent the incivility bug from contaminating your organization. Through coaching, you set expectations, sculpt civility, and create the norms for which people hold one another accountable. Scoring civility shows people that you take it seriously and that people will face serious consequences for behaving rudely. When your employees need work, motivate them to improve and help them practice. By working on all four of these steps, your organization won't just free itself of the scourge of incivility; it will reap the full benefits of a pervasive culture of kindness and respect. Of course, if someone isn't recyclable, don't compromise and harbor uncivil employees; it's just not worth it.

KEY POINTS

- Hone your employees' skills by giving corrective feedback. You must correct bad behavior quickly and firmly.

- Have the courage to take a stand no matter how talented your employees are. Don't let customers, clients, or suppliers treat your employees badly either.

- Treat people well on their way out.

- Follow up after people leave your organization. Exit interviews are best after about six months.

PART **IV**

Lift Yourself:
Handling Incivility
if *You're* the Target

So what do you do if you're targeted? Our final section addresses that question.

CHAPTER **14**

Your Antidote to Incivility

What does not destroy me, makes me stronger.
—Friedrich Nietzsche

At the beginning of this book, I described a woman I met in an elevator who was experiencing incivility in her workplace and was desperate for advice. At the time, I was unable to give her much help. I've often thought back on what I would have told her if I'd had the chance to frame a thoughtful answer. This chapter offers that advice. And it comes down to one core message: *Focus on yourself and your future.* When people mistreat you at work, you have to take control. The way to do that is to bet on yourself, not on your ability to change the offender or the organization in which you work.

Many get stuck wondering if and how they should address the offender. I'll provide simple guidelines to help you decide and prepare for a discussion. Before I get into that, though, let's cover a few basics that might help you pick up the pieces and feel better after being targeted.

Don't Just "Suck It Up"

If you report your uncivil treatment to someone else, you might hear them say things like "Suck it up," "Develop a thicker skin," "Don't let it bother you so much," or "Try to keep it in perspective." If any of this speaks to you and helps you move forward, then by all means use it. But this advice usually misses the mark because it fails to take into account that we are each hardwired differently; civility is in the eyes of the recipient.

Our brains differ in their sensitivities to adrenaline, serotonin, and other stress modulators and neurotransmitters. A study reported in *Science*, for instance, found that our genes largely determine whether stress in our lives will cause us to become depressed.[1] The serotonin transporter gene, 5-HTT, which helps regulate arousal, mood, sleep, and cognition, moderates the influence of stressful events on depression.[2] This gene also largely determines how we respond to threats, humiliation, loss, and defeat—all stimuli commonly associated with experiences of incivility.

Another important factor that determines how stressful incivility is for us is how much control or power we have over it.[3] If someone with more power than us treats us poorly, as nearly two-thirds of the time is the case, it hits us harder. Or if our boss's or our organization's norms force us to work with a toxic colleague, our sense of hopelessness increases. Countless lab studies on mice and people show that they really struggle when they experience stressors over which they lack control.[4] It's crucial that you fight those feelings of helplessness.

There's something else to consider: Are you a lefty or a righty? Your brain is divided into two hemispheres. The right side largely determines your response to negative feelings, such as fear, anxiety, and disgust.[5] When you experience positive feelings, such as joy, pride, hope, amusement, and love, the left side of your brain lights up. Some researchers suggest that people who have more activity on the right side—"cortical righties"—tend to be more depressed and more anxious. Lucky cortical lefties tend to be happier.[6]

The left side of your brain plays a key role in your ability to recover from incivility. While the amygdala is fanning the flames of fear and anxiety that incivility triggers, the left side of your brain acts like a fire extinguisher, exerting a calming influence. If you have stronger, quicker activity on the left side, you're likely to recover more quickly.[7] If you're a righty, you'll tend to be slower than a lefty to recover. And these differences in reaction are not necessarily small. Research has found that our ability to recover from incivility can vary as much as 3,000 percent among individuals.[8]

Don't Get Sucked In

Regardless of how sensitive you are, or how quickly you recover, you need to manage your response to incivility, both in the moment and shortly afterward. During this brief window of time, events can quickly spiral out of control, affecting both you and your career. Behave wisely. Remind yourself of what is at stake. Follow the cardinal rule: Don't get sucked in. Recognize that emotions are contagious and anger can escalate very quickly. Give yourself some space to decide what to do. And, above all, *avoid the temptation to get even.* Doing so will likely require you to stoop to the other person's level, which in turn might prove damaging to your reputation.

You might wonder if you should confront a rude colleague. I advise that you ask yourself three questions:

- Do I feel physically safe talking with the perpetrator?
- Was this behavior intentional?
- Is the offender's behavior unique?

The answers to these questions aren't always clear, especially when you're upset, so you might want to run the specifics of the answers by a colleague, family member, mentor, or friend. They might be better able to consider the perpetrator's situation and the larger organizational context.

If you answered yes to all three questions, then sit down with the perpetrator and discuss how his or her behavior made you feel. But prepare for the discussion before busting anyone's door down to talk. Think about a good time to meet and a safe environment in which you—and ideally both of you—will feel comfortable. Consider whether you will include other people as witnesses or mediators (e.g., human resources staff). Consider rehearsing; test your ideas and style with people who can give you honest feedback. Ask them to role-play the perpetrator, complete with the offender's temperament. Go in with a mindset of mutual gain. How can you both benefit from what you're going to share?

During the actual discussion, be sure to focus on the issue—not the individual—and how the specific behavior harms your and their performance. Use your listening skills. Be mindful of not only your words but also your nonverbal communication, especially your tone of voice. This, of course, is easier said than done, but that's because most people practice *what* they are going to say rather than *how* they will say it. Throughout your discussion, be mindful of your core posture, eye contact, facial expressions, natural gestures (nervous gestures, fidgeting), tempo, and timing of words. Be sure, as well, to read the offender's physical interaction and his or her nonverbals. If the perpetrator gets emotional or starts venting, try to tolerate it. Doing so may lead you to a more productive place, particularly if you acknowledge the perpetrator's feelings with phrases like "I get that" or "I understand." Admitting blame when appropriate can also be very helpful.

Finally, check in to show you are listening actively; paraphrase what you hear, and ask if they see things the same way. In experiments, I have found that people gain credibility and are perceived as more likeable when they ask humble questions this way. Remember, your goal in the discussion should be to identify and agree on norms for the future to increase effectiveness. So stay focused on better understanding their viewpoint. Does the uncivil colleague feel they were mistreated? Is there something outside the workplace—something completely unrelated—that has pulled them off track and distorted their ability to be civil and work effectively? This information will help a lot in moving forward.

Now, if you answered no to any of my previous questions, then do not *discuss the incident with them. Follow the acronym BIFF in your future encounters: Be* Brief, Informative, Friendly, *and* Firm.

Also,

- keep conversations pointed;
- minimize working face-to-face, steering clear of projects and committees if you can, working through the perpetrator's assistant, or working from other locations; and
- meet with the offender away from your own office—so that you can control the end of the meeting—preferably in a neutral setting.

Take Steps to Thrive

Above and beyond how you deal with the perpetrator, another factor can buffer civility's toxic effects: a sense of *thriving*. If you do nothing else, be sure to focus on yourself, cultivating an internal sense of being energized, alive, and growing. In studies conducted across a range of industries, I have found that people who experience a state of thriving are healthier, more resilient, and more able to focus on their work. When people feel even an inkling of thriving, it often buffers them from distractions, stress, and negativity. In a study of six organizations spanning six industries, employees characterized as highly thriving demonstrated 1.2 times less burnout compared with their peers.[9] High thrivers were 52 percent more confident in themselves and their ability to take control of a situation.[10] They were far less likely to have incivility drag them down a chute of negativity, distraction, or self-doubt.[11]

When you experience incivility, your sense of thriving comes into play in a particular way: by making it easier for you to reframe the negativity of the event so that it isn't nearly as destructive. One of my friends, a talented coach, likes to ask people faced with adversity, "What are you going to make this mean?" As he recognizes, how you interpret a situation is crucial. How much are you going to let someone pull you down? What useful lessons might there be for you in the situation?

Science reveals that about 50 percent of our happiness is based on brain wiring; 40 percent is owed to how we interpret and respond to what happens to us, and 10 percent is driven by our circumstances (e.g., whether we have less power; whether we're more dependent on the job or the offender, etc.).[12] In large part, you really do get to decide how you interpret incivility, the meaning you assign to it, and the stories you tell yourself. You also get to control whether it makes you feel bad or not. It may not be realistic for you to "toughen up," but you can *choose* not to worry about what was said or done to you.

If you're thriving, you're less likely to worry about the hit you took or to interpret words or deeds negatively. In fact, you're more likely to craft an interpretation that validates yourself and your behavior. People who focus more on thriving following an incident of incivility report that their performance suffered 34 percent less.[13] That's a big difference!

I've seen thriving's transformative effect in my own life. Earlier in this book, I mentioned how I felt when a senior person ripped on the title of my first book. I wasn't wedded to that title at all, but I was vulnerable. This person had more power than me; plus, I was up for a promotion, and not just any promotion: I would either get tenure or lose my job. Because of the general sense of thriving I felt in my life, I was aware that I had a choice. I could let this perpetrator's words eat me alive—or not. I could sit in front of my computer screen each day like a zombie, crumbling and teary-eyed in my seat, replaying the scenario over in my head, wallowing in self-pity, feeling bad about my abilities. I could let the incivility I'd experienced sink my self-esteem. I could ruminate on the what-ifs: *What will I do if this person destroys my career? Where will I go? How will I resurrect myself?* Or I could find a more productive way of responding.

If I let this guy's comments be about me and my work, I'd be toast. I'd be a fraction of myself on good days. Not only would my research wither away, but also I would become a mini-me in the classroom—a depressed, diminutive version of myself. My negative emotions would infect the MBAs and executives. Instead of presenting a fun, engaging class, peppered with dialogue and banter, I would stumble through it and freeze when tossed questions or challenges. I would also bring down my family and friends. I could try to rally, to "put on a happy, brave face," but it would be hard to hide this kind of hit. Those who know me well would be able to tell.

At the time, I was thriving in my life: I felt energized; I had a sense of growing, of moving toward something. And because I did, I could make the decision to interpret the situation in a way that affirmed my overall self-concept. I attributed the incident to the perpetrator, not to me. I decided to see his comments as reflecting *his* judgmental nature, not any performance deficiencies on my part. He was tearing people down rather than building them up, and there's no reason I had to feel bad.

Helping Yourself to Thrive

You might wonder whether it's possible to sustain a sense of thriving in the wake of a disturbing incident of incivility. Good news: It is! First, stop replaying the rude encounter in your mind. Try to limit the time you allow yourself to feel the hurt, injustice, or outrage that incivility often provokes. Tina Sung, a vice president at the nonprofit Partnership for Public Service, shared with me a saying that I love: "You can visit pity city, but you can't live there." Rituals such as journaling can help. In his recent book *The Road to Character*, David Brooks mentioned how former US president Dwight D. Eisenhower often furiously ranted in his journal as a way to release negative emotions related to colleagues (apparently he started the habit while working as an aide for the famously tyrannical general Douglas MacArthur). If you work out your anger, hurt, or frustration in writing, you're less likely to take it out on others and perpetuate a cycle of incivility.

In my case, I didn't need to journal. Instead, I asked myself, "Am I going to fight for my past or my future?" I have found that asking and answering this question helps me clearly commit to a game plan when I feel hurt or I've been treated unjustly. For me, this question presents me with a clear path forward. I *want* to move forward productively. I don't want to spend my life staring in the rearview mirror.

If, like me, you decide to focus on the future, then you can go further and reinforce your sense of thriving by focusing on personal growth and learning. There are a number of ways to do this:

1) Identify areas for growth and actively pursue development in those areas.

Researchers Teresa Amabile and Steven Kramer have shown that a sense of progress is the most powerful motivator in the workplace, even stronger than personal recognition or pay.[14] Feeling a sense of progress in virtually any area of your life will help you thrive. Kate, a young woman working in marketing, felt that "a toxic environment was chipping away at her soul," yet she did not see a path out of her position. She opted to pursue an MBA in an evening program. Little steps along the way, such as achieving a great GMAT score and meeting new colleagues, gave her a much-needed shot of confidence and joy. Instead of feeling shackled to a horrible environment, she felt a sense of growth and progress. She was rising. And while Kate didn't know where she would land, she felt stronger and more resilient by proactively pursuing growth.

2) Look for opportunities to innovate.

Find ways to contribute to projects that extend beyond your daily routine.[15] If immediate opportunities don't exist within the organization, seek leadership and learning opportunities in your local community, such as joining an organizational board. Honing a new skill, hobby, or sport can yield a sense of growth and progress. One friend decided to dust off his golf clubs, enroll in lessons, and hit the links. Being outdoors in a beautiful environment had a calming effect, reducing his stress. He felt good about the time he was taking for himself. Since he often golfed alone, he had the space he needed to process encounters with stressful work and challenging colleagues. He could think more clearly and develop better strategies. When he got back to the office, he felt more balanced and ready to take uncivil behavior in stride. And crushing the golf ball—well, that was fun too. He could take out his aggression, imagining his boss as that dimpled little ball. He was going to punish it as he swung for the green. In this way, golf became a helpful way for my friend to keep his anger in check and away from the office.

Start something that will make you feel like you're progressing, learning, or growing. You might volunteer to help newcomers or other coworkers. Choose something that makes you feel smarter, stronger, or more interesting, that clears your mind or feeds your soul.

3) Turn to a mentor.

Lynne, a consultant, benefitted from a mentor who helped her survive and thrive in an uncivil environment. This mentor wasn't afraid to question her and remind her of the toll the toxic environment had taken on her happiness, well-being, and productivity. Why didn't Lynne avoid events with people who upset her? Why pour energy into managing confrontations and conversations that would drain her spirit and productivity when she could often just as easily work from home? This mentor served as a role model for Lynne, helping her focus on navigating land mines that otherwise might have damaged her morale and career. Although she often found her mentor's advice challenging, and although she felt selfish at first about relying so heavily on her mentor's generosity, Lynne couldn't deny that the mentor's strategies and advice dramatically improved her well-being. Talking to a mentor also helped her performance, enabling her to score a big promotion.

4) Take good care of yourself by managing your energy.

We've talked about incivility as an infectious pathogen, a virus. Your defense against it depends to a large extent on your ability to manage your energy. My research suggests that many of the factors that help prevent illness—good nutrition, sleep, stress management—can also help ward off incivility's noxious effects (and prevent you from being uncivil, as discussed in chapter 5). Sleep is particularly important; research shows that the lack of it increases your susceptibility to distraction, robbing you of self-control in the face of rude colleagues. Sleep deprivation (usually defined as fewer than five hours a night) will almost certainly lead you to respond poorly to incivility, perhaps even in ways that hurt your career.[16]

As we saw in chapter 5, exercise helps us to behave in civil ways. It also helps us to respond better to incivility by enabling us to combat the anger, fear, and sadness that incivility typically causes. The more you exercise, the more you build up your cognitive potential and dump the unhelpful thoughts and emotions that weigh you down. One study of 1,632 workers found that those who exercised at least four hours a week were 50 percent less likely to suffer from depression or burnout.[17] Another study found that exercise was more effective than sertraline (Zoloft), a leading treatment for depression.[18] Those who regularly exercise are far less likely to sulk and far better able to rebound following negative interactions. So get moving!

Maintaining your energy in other ways, such as healthy eating, helps put you in tip-top form to respond well in the face of rudeness. How well do you respond to frustration when you're famished? Most of us tend to lash out; we lack the self-control required to respond patiently. Similarly, mindfulness—the shifting of your consciousness to process situations more slowly and thoughtfully and to respond more purposefully—can calm you when you're frustrated and primed to unleash on someone.

5) Find meaning or a sense of purpose.

In one study, I found that high-thriving individuals' worked more productively in uncivil teams, but their resilience was boosted even further when they engaged in work they considered meaningful.[19] So ask yourself, "How is my work meaningful?" To the extent that you can, take steps to shape your job into something that carries even more significance for you. Job crafting, a technique developed by scholars Justin Berg at Stanford, Jane Dutton at the University of Michigan, and Amy Wrzesniewski at Yale, is a great resource to help you generate more meaning at work by shaping your activities around your motives, strengths, and passions.[20] The exercise involves visualizing your job, mapping its elements, and reorganizing those elements to better suit your needs and personality.

Four strategies (that stem from Amy Wrzesniewski's work) can help you spark job crafting for you or your employees. Begin by reflecting on how you spend your time in the tasks, interactions, and relationships at work. Then

- optimize your current job by allocating time and energy differently so as to build a sense of control, positive identity, and connection with others;
- adapt your work to capitalize on positive, energizing interactions;
- reorder tasks and interactions to feed yourself and your sense of meaning, allowing you to engage more at key points in your day; and
- invest in your future by building a repertoire of skills or experiences that provide a path to more meaningful work.[21]

6) Seek positive relationships inside and outside work.

It's sad but true: Across industries, organizations, and levels, de-energizing relationships have four to seven times greater impact on an employee's sense of thriving than energizing, positive relationships.[22] To offset the effects of each de-energizer in your office, you should surround yourself with a small group of energizers. It's not difficult to identify energizers; they are the people in your life who make you smile and laugh, lifting your spirit. Spend more time with these folks. You might even tap into their network of friends.

7) Focus on thriving outside work.

In studies of MBAs, executive MBAs, and employees, I have found a consistently strong correlation between thriving outside work and thriving at work. Thriving in non-work activities doubles an individual's emotional reserves while instilling a sense of growth and learning. In a study of people who experienced incivility, those who reported thriving in non-work activities reported 80 percent better health, 89 percent greater thriving at work, and 38 percent more satisfaction with their handling of the incivility.[23] Seeking leadership opportunities in the community, particularly if such opportunities don't exist within your organization, bolsters both cognitive and affective thriving. Think about what will make you happier outside the office, and start doing it.

Should You Leave?

Thriving is really about trying to be the best version of yourself—energized, engaged, and with a sense of forward momentum and hunger for learning. Many of us can achieve this at work even in the face of incivility, but some may require a job change or relocation. Approximately one in eight people who report working in an uncivil environment ultimately end up leaving as a result. If you're thinking about leaving, weigh the following:

- How easily can I move to a better workplace?
- What would I gain or lose if I left?
- How would leaving affect my career?
- Is my current workplace destined to remain uncivil?
- Is incivility at work depleting my life outside work?
- Is workplace incivility injuring my self-image?
- Is incivility causing me stress?

Incivility is costly, but as we've seen, you can take steps to manage and minimize the toll it takes. Focus on yourself and your sense of thriving. Identify areas of growth and development and pursue them. Lean on a mentor, friends, or family. Take care of yourself and manage your energy. Look to enhance a sense of meaning or purpose in your work and life. Invest in positive relationships. Focus on your life outside work. As I can attest firsthand, doing some or all of these things will enable you to prevent incivility from eating away at your focus, your spirit, and your potential. You will thrive, not just survive.

Remember, you have a choice: What are you going to make this encounter with incivility mean? How are you going to respond? Who do you want to be? Are you going to cower or are you going to soar?

You have more control than you think. Your attitude, mindset, and willfulness can make all the difference. Don't let someone make you a smaller version of yourself. Take a deep breath. Gather yourself. Refuel. Stand tall. Play big. Don't you owe that to yourself?

KEY POINTS

- Spend time with energizers, the people in your life who make you smile and laugh.

- Stop ruminating. Try not to overanalyze a situation or engage in negative thinking about someone.

- Craft your job to be more meaningful. Leverage your strengths.

- Don't let incivility take a toll on your health. Exercise regularly, eat right, and get enough sleep.

Conclusion

Treat those around you with respect and dignity and they will thrive. Treat them with unkindness and they will fall apart.
—Richard Branson

Joe, a surgeon at a large California medical center, never thought of himself as a mean or abrasive person. But the nurses and residents who worked with him did. And in 2006, they told him so, responding to questions about his behavior in a 360 feedback review. They complained that Joe barked orders at them. He got angry. He didn't listen.

Joe was shocked and chagrined. But he was determined to change. For a few months, he paid close attention to his behavior. The toughest challenge was tempering his harsh tone. Initially, asking questions rather than barking orders didn't feel natural to him. Like others of his generation, he was used to surgeons adopting an authoritative "command and control" style. His mentors had done so with him. In tough, stressful moments, he slipped right back into this behavior.

As time passed, however, modifying his behavior became easier. He began to say hello to people more often—addressing them by name. He smiled more. He asked more questions, and even said thank you more often when people did as he asked.

Colleagues noticed. They started treating him differently,

smiling back at him instead of glaring. Teams he worked with perked up. They attacked their work more energetically, sharing more information and ideas. These developments motivated Joe to work even harder to behave civilly. A positive cycle kicked in, allowing everyone to focus more on their work and to serve patients better. Joe no longer infected people with the incivility bug. Instead, he injected them with positivity. The feedback about his behavior had been hard to take, but looking back on it a year later, he wished he had received it decades earlier.

Our behavior isn't fixed, cast in stone. All of us, no matter how we've behaved in the past, can improve. If we care the least bit about ourselves, our work, and our organizations, we *must* improve. So don't wait. Start today. Strive to listen more attentively. It's the foundation of mastering civility, the pathway toward healthy, meaningful, lasting relationships. Acknowledge people. Say hello. Smile more. Look to include others, especially those who are forgotten or who are in need of our understanding and help. Practice e-civility. Give more—of yourself and your resources (smartly, of course).

If it's never too late to embrace civility, it's never too early either. When twenty-one-year-old golf phenom Jordan Spieth won the Masters on April 12, 2015, he kindly thanked his hosts, the chairman and members of the Augusta National Golf Club, for "having us at this majestic place" in "a tournament like no other."[1] He lavished praise on the volunteers, telling them, "I couldn't have done it without you all. It's very underrated, what you guys do, the hours you put in, and we really do appreciate it." He acknowledged his caddy, saying, "You were the reason the dream came true and I really appreciate the work you put in, lots of hours that nobody can see.... You're the best, man. I appreciate it!" He thanked his instructor, trainer, and entire team, telling them that he respected what they did and put his "full trust in them." Last, but not least, he thanked his family and close friends for sharing the special moment with him.[2]

Conclusion

How many of us thank the people who serve us? Do we thank the caddies in our lives—the people behind the scenes who scout conditions and lay the groundwork for our success, who carry our bags, who support us when we fail?[3] Do we highlight the contributions of everyone on our team? Do we thank the people who make us smile?

Later in 2015, after a string of major tournament wins, Spieth had a chance to attempt something no golfer before him had been capable of: win the Masters, the US Open, the British Open, and the PGA Championship.[4] Spieth won the first two, but in the British Open he ended up falling just short late in his final round. What did Spieth do? He waited patiently for the winner, Zach Johnson, to finish up in a playoff. Then Spieth made sure to be one of the first people to hug and congratulate Johnson.

Whether celebrating competitors during or after rounds,[5] applauding fans, or thanking people, Spieth offers us an inspiring example of civility and sportsmanship. After his Masters win, his father, Shawn, acknowledged his son's golf prowess but said, "We're just probably more proud of him for the kind of person he is and the way he handles himself and treats everybody.... He makes us really, really proud."[6]

In the end, it's relationships that truly matter, and civility is the foundation of relationships. Respectful actions and gestures help us progress and gain influence in our careers, but they also help us connect with others and make a positive difference in their lives. Whether in business or in life, you can be civil *and* get ahead. Whatever your age or circumstance, you can master civility. So what are you doing today to connect with others? What kind of legacy are you leaving? Are you lifting people up or holding them down?

In each moment, we get to choose who we want to be.

Who do *you* want to be?

Acknowledgments

I've been blessed with family, friends, teachers, and communities who exude civility and have lifted me up. My grandparents served others and showered me with kindness. My parents exemplify to me what it is to give—and to treat people well. Aunts, uncles, and cousins inspire me. In particular, Ann McGowan Porath has spent decades advocating for equal justice for those in need. She and Jerry Porath have been role models. Pat and Terry Toepker fed my spirit with books. Terry and Hilde Clark motivate me with their giving.

Great teachers, especially those at Gilmour, shaped my future and my interests. Holy Cross instilled the Jesuit beliefs in me. My basketball coach, Bill Gibbons, was a role model who created a tight team and encouraged our involvement in the community. My experiences with Kolleen Rask and the Economics Honors Program gave me a taste for research and a desire to be a professor.

Professors and friends at the University of North Carolina at Chapel Hill, including Amy Kenworthy, Marcus Stewart, and Ian Williamson, shepherded me through the PhD program. Christine Pearson is a wonderful mentor. I have grown immensely from our work on incivility. Tom Bateman and Jane Dutton are great mentors who bestow advice. Jeff Edwards gave me a foundation in methodology.

I was fortunate to start my academic career at the University of Southern California. Ed Lawler, Warren Bennis, and Morgan

McCall were phenomenal role models who did meaningful research that has enlightened practice for decades. In particular, Ed continues to provide advice and support. Deborah MacInnis and Valerie Folkes are fantastic mentors I admire. I've really enjoyed uncovering how incivility affects both customers and marketing together.

I appreciate my experiences at Georgetown University, including the opportunity to work with talented students, executives, and alumni. Thanks to lab manager Christopher Hydock.

Thanks to Marga Biller, Michele Rigolizzo, and the wonderful executives in the Learning Innovations Laboratory (LILA) program at Harvard University for discussing this research, offering ideas, and sharing experiences. Thanks to Jo Solet for collaborating with me on how sleep is tied to civility. Thanks to Google for their re:work conferences and sharing their learning so generously on their re:work website.

The insights here were brought to life by thousands of individuals who described their work experiences to me. I am grateful for their candor, which has educated and inspired me for more than two decades.

I thank the organizations that opened their doors to me so that people could benefit. In particular, I'm grateful to Amy D'Ambra, Christine Rich, Laszlo Bock, Jennifer Kurkoski, Kathryn Dekas, Brian Welle, Tom Gardner, Lee Burbage, Brian Bjelde, Tim Tassopoulos, Jay Moldenhauer-Salazar, Stuart Price, Wendy Rice-Isaacs, Patrick Quinlan, Laura Hastings, Britta Wilson, Vicki Lostetter, Christina Fernandez, and Christopher Lu. I benefitted from discussions about how to foster civility with friends David Giuliano, Jeff McHenry, retired Justice Gary Hastings, Tina Sung, Tony Morgado, Raazi Imam, Lieutenant Christopher Manning, and Adam Mendler.

I appreciate the guiding hand of Lorin Rees, who stood by this idea for many years. Thanks for your unwavering encouragement from the very beginning and for leading me to Seth Schulman, a gifted editor whose suggestions consistently added value; I have been very fortunate to work with him.

I am deeply grateful to Gretchen Young and Grand Central Publishing for believing in and championing the project. It has been an honor to work with extraordinary editor Katherine Stopa. Katherine provided exceptional feedback and wonderful support throughout the process. My thanks go to Dianna Stirpe for her excellent copy editing. Thanks to many others at Grand Central Publishing who invested themselves in this book. I appreciate all the work you've done! Thanks to Ed Klaris for his suggestions and wise counsel.

I am appreciative of the collaborative opportunities I have shared with other colleagues whose efforts have informed my understanding of workplace civility, including Amir Erez, Alexandra Gerbasi, Sebastian Schorch, and Jessica Kennedy. Thanks goes to collaborators on other projects, including Tony Schwartz, Gretchen Spreitzer, Cristina Gibson, Robert Cross, Kristin Cullen-Lester, Andrew Parker, and Trevor Foulk.

Thank you to friends at the *Harvard Business Review*—Amy Gallo, Eben Harrell, Ellen Peebles, Sarah Green, and others—who helped shape my work and have provided many opportunities for this work to have an impact. Thanks to Trish Hall and the *New York Times* for giving me opportunities to share my research.

Thanks to Greg Long, Mark Kennedy, Bailey O'Donnell, Craig Rubens, Anna Fraser, Kimberly Perttula, Amy Wrzesniewski, Valeria Khislavsky, and Dax Alvarez for your helpful advice, assistance, and encouragement along the way. Thanks to Yahya Cheema for his help with the online civility test. Thanks to Heather Ahearn, Lauren George, and Mary Mulligan for their friendship. I'm very grateful to Adam Grant, who kindly shared his wisdom every step of the way.

I am incredibly grateful to my family—my parents, Mark Porath, Carrie and Tripp Cherry, and Sarah Porath—and close

Acknowledgments

friends for their support. They are always lifting me up and making me smile! Finally, my deepest thanks go to my brother, Mike Porath. Mike provided editing and many ideas that shaped this book. He was always there to provide advice and support even while he was building The Mighty. Thank you!

Tools: Additional Actions to Become Your Best, Most Civil Self

Manage your energy. Take a brief assessment (http://the energyproject.com/audits/individual) to see how well you're managing your area and where you could improve most. Consider doing an energy audit (http://positiveorgs.bus.umich.edu/wp-content /uploads/GrantSpreitzer-EnergyAudit.pdf) to see how and when your energy ebbs and flows. Make adjustments. You might tailor your work (and challenging situations!) accordingly.

Learn from excellent role models. Think about some excellent examples of civility. Who are the people you respect most? Also think about leaders you've encountered who exemplify civility. Think about other people you've witnessed who are role models for civility and, more generally, represent how you would like to be perceived.

- List several of these people on a piece of paper. Label what each person does, specifically, that leads you to feel this way.
- In each of your examples, compare your analysis of the person to how you behave. What elements are similar? In which areas do you fall short? What qualities might you adopt to improve?

Evaluate your biases. Take the complete Implicit Association Test (https://implicit.harvard.edu/implicit/takeatest.html) to find out how you stack up.

Evaluate your interpersonal skills.

Take a body language test.

- Researchers use the Interpersonal Reactivity Index to test empathy and other responses to others' behaviors.
- Test your emotional intelligence at the Greater Good Science Center (http://greatergood.berkeley.edu/ei_quiz/).

Practice your listening skills. Julian Treasure, author and TED speaker on conscious listening recommends

- **Silence**: Practice being silent for three minutes a day to reset your ears.
- **Mixture**: Even in an extremely noisy environment, focus on how many channels of sound you hear. This improves the quality of your listening.
- **Savoring**: Practice savoring various sounds ("the hidden choir"), from the mundane to the sounds you cherish.
- **Listening positions**: Though there are many, practice a variety of listening positions, such as active vs. passive, reductive vs. expansive, and critical vs. empathetic.

Actions and Impact for Your Group and Organization

Who's (Civil) in Your Group?

In your group, provide feedback to one another. Begin by giving each individual in the group a copy of the following list of behaviors. Each person should mark who in your group does each behavior, writing group members' names in the columns. Check who comes to mind for each of the behaviors. You can select more than one person (and include yourself). If nobody fits the item, leave it blank. Then, after everyone has done the task individually, meet in a group and share the feedback. This can be done item by item, or the list can be used as a resource to provide feedback on strengths and areas for improvement for each group member.

Names						
Says please and thank you						
Passes the blame when he or she has contributed to a mistake						
Smiles						
Uses e-mail when face-to-face communication is needed						
Acknowledges others						
Takes too much credit for collaborative work						
E-mails or texts during meetings						

Actions and Impact for Your Group and Organization

Keeps people waiting needlessly						
Talks down to others						
Speaks kindly of others						
Delays access to information or resources						
Uses jargon even when it excludes others						
Spreads rumors about others						
Belittles others nonverbally (e.g., rolls his or her eyes, smirks)						
Hibernates into his or her e-gadgets						
Makes people feel a part of a network or team						
Shuts someone out of a network or team						
Is a giver (e.g., shares resources, helps others)						
Takes advantage of others						
Pays little attention or shows little interest in others' opinions						
Listens well						
Looks out for others						
Sets others up for failure						
Shows up late or leaves a meeting early with no explanation						
Insults others						
Belittles others and their efforts						
Makes demeaning or derogatory remarks to someone						
Takes others' contributions for granted						
Grabs easy tasks while leaving difficult ones for others						

Is civil in e-mails						
Is respectful when disagreeing						
Interrupts others						
Judges people who are different from him or her						
Appreciates others' efforts						

Discussion Questions for Your Team or Organization

1. What do civility and incivility look like in our team/ organization?
2. What effect does incivility have on individuals/employees? Our team? Our organization? Other stakeholders (e.g., clients, customers, investors)?
3. How does civility affect individuals/employees? Our team? Our organization? Other stakeholders (e.g., clients, customers, investors)?
4. How am I a carrier of the incivility bug? Who do I infect at work? Outside work? Who does incivility touch, even if I don't want it to? Who pays? How?
5. What am I doing and saying that spreads civility? What are the ripple effects?
6. What's the biggest blind spot of each teammate? (Give each other pointed feedback.)
7. What biases do we carry individually, or as a team?
8. How do these biases creep into our interactions? (Your non-verbals may tell the story.)
9. Are there certain people or groups we are disadvantaging?

10. What can we do to break the caste system in our organization or team? How can we be more inclusive? (Consider pleasantries, events, and other ideas to make others feel like part of the team.)
11. Might we be getting less from someone because we expect less from them?
12. What do we want our norms to be in our team/organization?
13. Are we willing to hold one another accountable for our norms (of civility)?

Guiding Questions for Coaching Civility

Specifically, these guiding questions are to assess a manager who tends to belittle:

- *What* does the belittling behavior consist of? Does he shoot someone down in a meeting?
- *Whom* does he belittle? A subordinate? His entire team? Peers who may be gunning for the same promotion?
- *When* and *where* does this occur? In front of others? During one-on-one meetings? When his back is against the wall? During stressful moments?
- *How* does the belittling behavior affect others? Do they respond? Does it take them off track? Does it destroy their confidence? Does it make them less motivated to work with or for you?
- *Why* might he behave like this? Does he get pleasure out of it? Does it make him feel powerful? Is he very stressed at home? Is his job on the line?

Notes

Chapter 1: Clueless

1. Weber Shandwick, "Nearly All Likely Voters Say Candidates' Civility Will Affect Their Vote; New Poll Finds 93% Say Behavior Will Matter," press release, January 28, 2016, http://www.webershandwick.com/news /article/nearly-all-likely-voters-say-candidates-civility-will-affect-their-vote.
2. J. Zaslow, "The Most-Praised Generation Goes to Work," *Wall Street Journal*, April 20, 2007, http://www.wsj.com/articles/SB117702894815776259. Note that these were measured by standard personality inventories.
3. C. A. Bartel, A. Wrzesniewski, and B. M. Wiesenfeld, "Knowing Where You Stand: Physical Isolation, Perceived Respect, and Organizational Identification Among Virtual Employees," *Organization Science* 23, no. 3 (2012): 743–57.
4. R. Putnam, *Bowling Alone: The Collapse and Revival of American Community* (New York: Simon & Schuster, 2001); and M. J. Dunkelman, *The Vanishing Neighbor: The Transformation of American Community* (New York: W. W. Norton, 2014).
5. C. L. Porath, "No Time to Be Nice at Work," *Sunday Review, New York Times*, June 19, 2015, http://www.nytimes.com/2015/06/21/opinion/sunday/is-your -boss-mean.html?_r=0.
6. K. Narragon, "Subject: Email, We Just Can't Get Enough," *Adobe News* (blog), http://blogs.adobe.com/conversations/2015/08/email.html.

Chapter 2: Sidelined

1. R. M. Sapolsky, *Why Zebras Don't Get Ulcers*, 3rd ed. (New York: Owl Books / Henry Holt, 2004).
2. N. Slopen, R. J. Glynn, J. E. Buring, T. T. Lewis, D. R. Williams, et al. (2012), "Job Strain, Job Insecurity, and Incident Cardiovascular Disease in the Women's Health Study: Results from a 10-Year Prospective Study," *PLoS ONE* 7(7): e40512. doi: 10.1371/journal.pone.0040512.

Notes

3. J. Lehrer, "Your Co-Workers Might Be Killing You," *Wall Street Journal*, August 20, 2011, http://www.wsj.com/articles/SB10001424053111903392 904576512233116576352.

4. A. Shirom et al., "Work-Based Predictors of Mortality: A 20-Year Follow-Up of Healthy Employees," *Health Psychology* 30, no. 3 (2011): 268–75.

5. Lehrer, "Your Co-Workers Might Be Killing You," http://www.wsj.com /articles/SB10001424053111903392904576512233116576352.

6. S. Lim, L. M. Cortina, and V. J. Magley, "Personal and Workgroup Incivility: Impact on Work and Health Outcomes," *Journal of Applied Psychology* 93, no. 1 (2008): 95–107.

7. M. Ferguson, "You Cannot Leave It at the Office: Spillover and Crossover of Coworker Incivility," *Journal of Organizational Behavior* 33, no. 4 (2011): 571–88.

8. S. Lim and K. Tai, "Family Incivility and Job Performance: A Moderated Mediation Model of Psychological Distress and Core Self-Evaluation," *Journal of Applied Psychology* 99, no. 2 (2014): 351–59.

9. "Stress in America: Paying with Our Health," survey, American Physiological Association, February 4, 2015, http://www.apa.org/news/press/releases /stress/2014/stress-report.pdf.

10. E. Seppala and K. Cameron, "Proof That Positive Work Cultures Are More Productive," *Harvard Business Review* online, December 1, 2015; and Humana, "Combat Stress at Work to Promote Health," Focus, April 2009, http://apps.humana.com/marketing/documents.asp?file=1143441.

11. "Highlights: Workplace Stress and Anxiety Disorders Survey," Anxiety and Depression Association of America website, 2006, http://www.adaa .org/workplace-stress-anxiety-disorders-survey.

12. C. Pearson and C. Porath, *The Cost of Bad Behavior: How Incivility Is Damaging Your Business and What to Do About It* (New York: Portfolio / Penguin Group, 2009); and C. Porath and C. Pearson, "The Price of Incivility," *Harvard Business Review*, January–February 2013.

13. W. Cascio and J. Boudreau, *Investing in People: Financial Impact of Human Resource Initiatives* (Upper Saddle River, NJ: FT Press, 2008).

14. J. Connelly, "Have We Become Mad Dogs in the Office?" *Fortune*, November 28, 1994, 197–99.

15. C. L. Porath, D. J. MacInnis, and V. S. Folkes, "Witnessing Incivility Among Employees: Effects on Consumer Anger and Negative Inferences About Companies," *Journal of Consumer Research* 37, no. 2 (2010): 292–303.

16. Porath, MacInnis, and Folkes, "Witnessing Incivility Among Employees: Effects on Consumer Anger and Negative Inferences About Companies," *Journal of Consumer Research* 37, no. 2 (2010): 292–303.

Notes

17. C. L. Porath, D. J. MacInnis, and V. S. Folkes, "It's Unfair: Why Customers Who Merely Observe an Uncivil Employee Abandon the Company," *Journal of Service Research* 14, no. 3 (2011): 302–17.

18. C. L. Porath and A. Erez, "Does Rudeness Really Matter? The Effects of Rude Behavior on Task Performance and Helpfulness," *Academy of Management Journal* 50, no. 5 (2007): 1181–97.

19. C. L. Porath and A. Erez, "Overlooked but Not Untouched: How Rudeness Reduces Onlookers' Performance on Routine and Creative Tasks," *Organizational Behavior and Human Decision Processes* 109, no. 1 (2009): 29–44.

20. A. Erez, C. L. Porath, and T. Foulk, "Even if It's Only on Your Mind: The Cognitive Toll of Incivility" (working paper, University of Florida, Gainesville, 2007).

21. C. Chabris and D. Simons, *The Invisible Gorilla: And Other Ways Our Intuitions Deceive Us* (New York: Crown, 2010).

22. A. H. Rosenstein and M. O'Daniel, "A Survey of the Impact of Disruptive Behaviors and Communication Defects on Patient Safety," *Joint Commission Journal on Quality and Patient Safety* 34, no. 8 (2008): 464–71.

23. O. MacDonald. Disruptive physician behavior. May 15, 2011. Available at: www.quantiamd.com/q-qcp/Disruptive_Physician_Behavior.pdf. Accessed April 21, 2016.

24. A. Riskin et al., "The Impact of Rudeness on Medical Team Performance: A Randomized Trial," *Pediatrics* 136, no. 3 (2015): 487–95.

25. C. Porath, "How Civility Matters for You and Your Network," *The Water Cooler* (blog), Google re:Work, December 7, 2015, https://rework.withgoogle.com/blog/how-civility-matters-for-you-and-your-network/.

26. Porath and Erez, "Does Rudeness Really Matter?" 1181–97; Porath and Erez, "Overlooked but Not Untouched," 29–44; and C. L. Porath, "No Time to Be Nice at Work," *Sunday Review, New York Times*, June 19, 2015, http://www.nytimes.com/2015/06/21/opinion/sunday/is-your-boss-mean.html?_r=0.

27. Porath and Erez, "Overlooked but Not Untouched," 29–44.

Chapter 3: Civility Buys Everything

1. Terri Kelly, interview by Jeremy Hobson, "What It's Like to Lead a Non-Hierarchical Workplace," *Here and Now*, WBUR, July 1, 2015, http://hereandnow.wbur.org/2015/07/01/wl-gore-ceo-terri-kelly.

2. A. Deutschman, "The Un-CEO," *Fast Company*, September 1, 2005, http://www.fastcompany.com/53896/un-ceo; and "Gore CEO Terri Kelly Featured in Fast Company Magazine," press release, W. L. Gore and Associates, August 24, 2005, http://www.gore.com/en_xx/news/corp_fastcompany_terrikelly_050824.html.

3. N. Machiavelli, *The Prince and Other Writings*, trans. W. A. Rebhorn (New York: Barnes & Noble Books, 2003).

4. C. L. Porath, "No Time to Be Nice at Work," *Sunday Review, New York Times*, June 19, 2015, http://www.nytimes.com/2015/06/21/opinion /sunday/is-your-boss-mean.html?_r=0.

5. C. Porath, A. Gerbasi, and S. Schorch, "The Effects of Civility on Advice, Leadership, and Performance," *Journal of Applied Psychology* 100, no. 5 (2015): 1527–41; and C. Porath and A. Gerbasi, "Does Civility Pay?" *Organizational Dynamics* 44, no. 4 (2015): 281–86.

6. J. Kennedy and C. L. Porath, "Civility, Status, and Power" (working paper, Vanderbilt University, Nashville, 2015); and Machiavelli, *The Prince and Other Writings*.

7. Kennedy and Porath, "Civility, Status, and Power" (working paper, Vanderbilt University, Nashville, 2015).

8. Porath, Gerbasi, and Schorch, "The Effects of Civility on Advice, Leadership, and Performance," 1527–41; and Porath and Gerbasi, "Does Civility Pay?" 281–86.

9. T. Casciaro and M. S. Lobo, "When Competence Is Irrelevant: The Role of Interpersonal Affect in Task-Related Ties," *Administrative Science Quarterly* 53, no. 4 (2008): 655–84; and M. S. Lobo and T. Casciaro, "Competent Jerks, Lovable Fools, and the Formation of Social Networks," *Harvard Business Review*, June 2005.

10. Porath and Gerbasi, "Does Civility Pay?" 281–86. In one biotech firm we studied, the people viewed as civil had 1.5 times more energizing ties (i.e., people were energized to work with them) than those seen as uncivil. The people seen as uncivil had three times as many de-energizing ties (i.e., they had an enduring, recurring set of negative judgments, feelings, and behavioral intentions toward another person) as those seen as civil.

11. Porath and Gerbasi, "Does Civility Pay?" 281–86.

12. C. Porath, "How Civility Matters for You and Your Network," *The Water Cooler* (blog), Google re:Work, December 7, 2015, https://rework.withgoogle .com/blog/how-civility-matters-for-you-and-your-network/.

13. Porath, Gerbasi, and Schorch, "The Effects of Civility on Advice, Leadership, and Performance," 1527–41; and Porath and Gerbasi, "Does Civility Pay?" 281–86.

14. J. M. Kouzes and B. Z. Posner, *Credibility: How Leaders Gain and Lose It, Why People Demand It*, 2nd ed. (San Francisco: Jossey-Bass, 2011).

15. C. Porath, "The Leadership Behavior That's Most Important to Employees," Emotional Intelligence series, *Harvard Business Review* online, May 11, 2015, https://hbr.org/2015/05/the-leadership-behavior-thats-most-important -to-employees.

Notes

16. A. M. Koenig et al., "Are Leader Stereotypes Masculine? A Meta-Analysis of Three Research Paradigms," *Psychological Bulletin* 137, no. 4 (2011): 616–42.
17. W. Levinson et al., " Physician-Patient Communication. The Relationship with Malpractice Claims Among Primary Care Physicians and Surgeons," *Journal of the American Medical Association* 277, no. 7 (1997): 553–59.
18. N. Ambady et al., "Surgeons' Tone of Voice: A Clue to Malpractice History," *Surgery* 132, no. 1 (2002): 5–9.
19. M. Gladwell, *Blink: The Power of Thinking Without Thinking* (New York: Back Bay Books, 2005).
20. T. Qiu et al., "The Effect of Interactional Fairness on the Performance of Cross-Functional Product Development Teams: A Multilevel Mediated Model," *Journal of Product Innovation Management* 26, no. 2 (2009): 173–87.
21. A. Carmeli, J. E. Dutton, and A. E. Hardin, "Respect as an Engine for New Ideas: Linking Respectful Engagement, Relational Information Processing, and Creativity Among Employees and Teams," *Human Relations* 68, no. 6 (2015): 1021–47.
22. T. J. Vogus, "Mindful Organizing: Establishing and Extending the Foundations of Highly Reliable Performance," in *The Oxford Handbook of Positive Organizational Scholarship*, ed. K. Cameron and G. M. Spreitzer (Oxford, United Kingdom: Oxford University Press, 2011), 664–76.
23. L. Ramarajan, S. G. Barsade, and O. Burack, "The Influence of Organizational Respect on Emotional Exhaustion in the Human Services," *Journal of Positive Psychology* 3, no. 1 (2008): 4–18.
24. "Costco vs. Wal-Mart: Higher Wages Mean Superior Returns for Investors," http://www.fool.com/investing/general/2014/03/12/costco-vs-wal-mart-higher-wages-mean-superior-retu.aspx.
25. A.B. Goldberg and B. Ritter, "Costco CEO Finds Pro-Worker Means Profitability," *ABC News* August 2, 2006, http://abcnews.go.com/2020/Business/story?id=1362779.
26. W. Cascio, "The High Cost of Low Wages," *Harvard Business Review*, December 2006.
27. T. Schwartz and C. Porath, "Why You Hate Work," *Sunday Review, New York Times*, May 30, 2014, http://www.nytimes.com/2014/06/01/opinion/sunday/why-you-hate-work.html.
28. Porath, Gerbasi, and Schorch, "The Effects of Civility on Advice, Leadership, and Performance," 1527–41.
29. Porath, "The Leadership Behavior That's Most Important to Employees," https://hbr.org/2015/05/the-leadership-behavior-thats-most-important-to-employees.

30. Porath, "How Civility Matters for You and Your Network," https://rework
.withgoogle.com/blog/how-civility-matters-for-you-and-your-network/.

31. J. Rozovsky, "The Five Keys to a Successful Team," *The Water Cooler* (blog),
Google re:Work, November 17, 2015, https://rework.withgoogle.com
/blog/five-keys-to-a-successful-google-team/.

32. I. Mochari, "How Market Basket's Deposed CEO Earned Employee Loy-
alty," *Inc.*, July 25, 2014, http://www.inc.com/ilan-mochari/market-basket
-loyalty.html.

33. O. Khazan, "It Pays to Be Nice," *Atlantic*, June 23, 2015, http://www
.theatlantic.com/business/archive/2015/06/it-pays-to-be-nice/396512/;
and Mochari, "How Market Basket's Deposed CEO Earned Employee Loy-
alty," http://www.inc.com/ilan-mochari/market-basket-loyalty.html.

34. Khazan, "It Pays to Be Nice," http://www.theatlantic.com/business
/archive/2015/06/it-pays-to-be-nice/396512/.

35. C. Ross, "Arthur T. Demoulas Happy 'Just Being a Grocer,'" *Boston Globe*,
September 12, 2014, https://www.bostonglobe.com/business/2014/09/11
/after-epic-market-basket-battle-arthur-demoulas-happy-just-being-grocer
/Iqd3AyAX6qh36fhldPOyPN/story.html.

36. Morgan McCall, correspondence with author, June 18, 2015; and M. W.
McCall Jr. and M.M. Lombardo, "What makes a top executive?," *Psychology Today*, 2 (1983): 26-31.

Chapter 4: The Incivility Bug

1. N. A. Christakis and J. H. Fowler, *Connected: The Surprising Power of Our
Social Networks and How They Shape Our Lives* (New York: Little, Brown,
2009).

2. P. Totterdell, "Mood Scores: Mood and Performance in Professional Crick-
eters," *British Journal of Psychology* 90, no. 3 (1999): 317–32.

3. T. Foulk, A. Erez, and A. Woolum, "Catching Rudeness Is like Catching a
Cold: The Contagion Effects of Low-Intensity Negative Behaviors," *Journal
of Applied Psychology* 101, no. 1 (2016): 50–67.

4. Foulk, Erez, and Woolum, "Catching Rudeness Is like Catching a Cold,"
50–67; and C. L. Porath, T. Foulk, and A. Erez, "How Incivility Hijacks
Performance: It Robs Cognitive Resources, Increases Dysfunctional Behavior, and Infects Team Dynamics and Functioning," *Organizational Dynamics* 44, no. 4 (2015): 258–65.

5. M. L. Stanley et al., "Defining Nodes in Complex Brain Networks," *Frontiers
in Computation Neuroscience* 7 (2013): 169, doi:10.3389/fncom.2013.00169.

6. E. F. Loftus and J. C. Palmer, "Reconstruction of Automobile Destruction:
An Example of the Interaction Between Language and Memory," *Journal
of Learning and Verbal Behavior* 13, no. 5 (1974): 585–89; and S. McLeod,

"Loftus and Palmer," Simple Psychology website, last modified 2014, http://www.simplypsychology.org/loftus-palmer.html.

7. C. Carver et al., "Modeling: An Analysis in Terms of Category Accessibility," *Journal of Experimental Social Psychology* 19, no. 5 (1983): 403–21.

8. C. L. Porath, "No Time to Be Nice at Work," *Sunday Review, New York Times*, June 19, 2015, http://www.nytimes.com/2015/06/21/opinion/sunday/is-your -boss-mean.html?_r=0.

9. J. A. Bargh, M. Chen, and L. Burrows, "Automaticity of Social Behavior: Direct Effects of Trait Construct and Stereotype Activation on Action," *Journal of Personality and Social Psychology* 71, no. 2 (1996): 230–44.

10. E. M. Hallowell, *Worry* (New York: Random House, 1997).

11. L. W. Barsalou et al., "Social Embodiment," *Psychology of Learning and Motivation* 43 (2003): 43–92.

12. B. Hathaway, "Do the Math: Why Some People Are Jerks yet Others Are Even Nice to Strangers," *YaleNews*, January 11, 2016, http://news.yale .edu/2016/01/11/research-news-do-math-why-some-people-are-jerks-yet -others-are-even-nice-strangers; and A. Bear and D. G. Rand, "Intuition, Deliberation, and the Evolution of Cooperation," *Proceedings of the National Academy of Sciences* 113, no. 4 (2016): 936–41.

13. C. L. Porath et al., "Civility as an Enabler of Social Capital: How It Spreads—and What Limits Its Potential" (working paper, Georgetown University, Washington, DC, 2016).

14. Porath, "No Time to Be Nice at Work," http://www.nytimes.com/2015/06/21/ opinion/sunday/is-your-boss-mean.html?_r=0; and C. Porath and C. Pearson, "The Price of Incivility: Lack of Respect in the Workplace Hurts Morale—and the Bottom Line," *Harvard Business Review*, January–February 2013, 115–21.

Chapter 5: Are You Civil?

1. B. McGill, "Toward a Civil and Sane World," BryantMcGill.com, http:// bryantmcgill.com/20131201130106.html.

2. M. Goldsmith with M. Reiter, *What Got You Here Won't Get You There* (New York: Hyperion, 2007).

3. F. Gino, *Sidetracked* (Cambridge, MA: Harvard Business Review Press, 2013); and S. Vozza, "The Science Behind Our Self-Defeating Behavior," *Fast Company*, January 14, 2014, http://www.fastcompany.com/3024781 /leadership-now/the-science-behind-our-self-defeating-behavior.

4. A full version of this quiz is available online.

5. C. Porath, "Take the Assessment," Cycle to Civility website, http://cycleto civility.com/take-the-assessment; and C. Porath, "How Civility Matters for You and Your Network," *The Water Cooler* (blog), Google re:Work, December

7, 2015, https://rework.withgoogle.com/blog/how-civility-matters-for-you-and-your-network/.

6. Porath, "How Civility Matters for You and Your Network," https://rework.withgoogle.com/blog/how-civility-matters-for-you-and-your-network/.

7. C. Porath, "Quiz: How Toxic Is Your Work Environment?" *Sunday Review, New York Times,* June 19, 2015.

8. M. J. Poulin, E. A. Holman, and A. Buffone, "The Neurogenetics of Nice: Receptor Genes for Oxytocin and Vasopressin Interact with Threat to Predict Prosocial Behavior," *Psychological Science* 23, no. 5 (2012): 446–52, http://pss.sagepub.com/content/early/2012/03/28/0956797611428471.abstract.

9. C. Porath, "The Leadership Behavior That's Most Important to Employees," Emotional Intelligence series, *Harvard Business Review* online, May 11, 2015, https://hbr.org/2015/05/the-leadership-behavior-thats-most-important-to-employees.

10. A. Pentland, "Honest Signals: How They Shape Our World (Boston: MIT Press, 2008).; and A. Pentland, "To Signal is Human," *American Scientist* 90 (May–June 2010), http://web.media.mit.edu/~sandy/2010-05Pentland.pdf.

11. A. Mehabrian, *Nonverbal Communication* (Piscataway, NJ: Aldine Transaction, 2007).

12. D. Stone and S. Heen, *Thanks for the Feedback: The Science and Art of Receiving Feedback Well* (New York: Viking, 2014).

13. Stone and Heen, *Thanks for the Feedback.*

14. Stone and Heen, *Thanks for the Feedback.*

15. Stone and Heen, *Thanks for the Feedback.*

16. L. M. Roberts et al., "Composing the Reflected Best-Self Portrait: Building Pathways for Becoming Extraordinary in Work Organizations," *Academy of Management Review* 30, no. 4 (2005): 712–36; and L. M. Roberts et al., "How to Play to Your Strengths," *Harvard Business Review,* January 2005, 75–80.

17. Goldsmith with Reiter, *What Got You Here Won't Get You There.*

18. Porath, "The Leadership Behavior That's Most Important to Employees," https://hbr.org/2015/05/the-leadership-behavior-thats-most-important-to-employees.

19. Goldsmith with Reiter, *What Got You Here Won't Get You There.*

20. Porath, "The Leadership Behavior That's Most Important to Employees," https://hbr.org/2015/05/the-leadership-behavior-thats-most-important-to-employees; and C. Pearson and C. Porath, *The Cost of Bad Behavior: How Incivility Is Damaging Your Business and What to Do About It* (New York: Portfolio / Penguin Group, 2009).

21. "Empathy: What Is Empathy?" Greater Good Science Center, University of California, Berkeley, http://greatergood.berkeley.edu/topic/empathy /definition#what_is.

22. "Empathy: What Is Empathy?" http://greatergood.berkeley.edu/topic /empathy/definition#what_is.

23. "Empathy: What Is Empathy?" http://greatergood.berkeley.edu/topic /empathy/definition#what_is.

24. "Empathy: What Is Empathy?" http://greatergood.berkeley.edu/topic /empathy/definition#what_is.

25. Porath, "The Leadership Behavior That's Most Important to Employees," https://hbr.org/2015/05/the-leadership-behavior-thats-most-important-to -employees.

26. C. L. Porath, "No Time to Be Nice at Work," *Sunday Review, New York Times*, June 19, 2015, http://www.nytimes.com/2015/06/21/opinion /sunday/is-your-boss-mean.html?_r=0.

27. J. J. Ratey with E. Hagerman, *Spark: The Revolutionary New Science of Exercise and the Brain* (New York: Little, Brown, 2008).

28. S. E. Luckhaupt, S. Tak, and G. M. Calvert, "The Prevalence of Short Sleep Duration by Industry and Occupation in the National Health Interview Survey," *Sleep* 33, no. 2 (2010): 149–59.

29. S. Park et al., "Relationships of Sleep Duration with Sociodemographic and Health-Related Factors, Psychiatric Disorders and Sleep Disturbances in a Community Sample of Korean Adults," *Journal of Sleep Research* 19, no. 4 (2010): 567–77; A. R. Ravan et al., "Thirty-Six-Year Secular Trends in Sleep Duration and Sleep Satisfaction, and Associations with Mental Stress and Socioeconomic Factors—Results of the Population Study of Women in Gothenburg, Sweden," *Journal of Sleep Research* 19, no. 3 (2010): 496–503; S. Salminen et al., "Sleep Disturbances as a Predictor of Occupational Injuries Among Public Sector Workers," *Journal of Sleep Research* 19, no. 1 pt. 2 (2010): 207–13; and H. Westerlund et al., "Work-Related Sleep Disturbances and Sickness Absence in the Swedish Working Population, 1993–1999," *Sleep* 31, no. 8 (2008): 1169–77.

30. S. J. Banks et al., "Amygdala-Frontal Connectivity During Emotion Regulation," *Social Cognitive and Affective Neuroscience* 2, no. 4 (2007): 303–12; M. D. Beaumont et al., "Slow Release Caffeine and Prolonged (64-h) Continuous Wakefulness: Effects on Vigilance and Cognitive Performance," *Journal of Sleep Research* 10, no. 4 (2001): 265–76; L. Y. M. Chuah et al., "Sleep Deprivation and Interference by Emotional Distractors," *Sleep* 33, no. 10 (2010): 1305–13; J. P. Nilsson et al., "Less Effective Executive Functioning After One Night's Sleep Deprivation," *Journal of Sleep Research* 14, no. 1 (2005): 1–6; and K. N. Ochsner et al., "For Better or for Worse:

Neural Systems Supporting the Cognitive Down- and Up-Regulation of Negative Emotion," *Neuroimage* 23, no. 2 (2004): 483–99.

31. M. T. Gailliot et al., "Self-Control Relies on Glucose as a Limited Energy Source: Willpower Is More than a Metaphor," *Journal of Personality and Social Psychology* 92, no. 2 (2007): 325–36; and S. H. Fairclough and K. Houston, "A Metabolic Measure of Mental Effort," *Biological Psychology* 66, no. 2 (2004): 177–90.

32. M. Thomas et al., "Neural Basis of Alertness and Cognitive Performance Impairments During Sleepiness. I. Effects of 24 h of Sleep Deprivation on Waking Human Regional Brain Activity," *Journal of Sleep Research* 9, no. 4 (2000): 335–52.

33. N. van Dam and E. van der Helm, "The Organizational Cost of Insufficient Sleep," *McKinsey Quarterly*, February 2016, http://www.mckinsey .com/business-functions/organization/our-insights/the-organizational -cost-of-insufficient-sleep#0.

34. E. van der Helm, N. Gujar, and M. P. Walker, "Sleep Deprivation Impairs the Accurate Recognition of Human Emotions," *Sleep* 33, no. 3 (2010): 335–42; and E. van der Helm et al., "REM Sleep De-Potentiates Amygdala Activity to Previous Emotional Experiences," *Current Biology* 21, no. 23 (2011): 2029–32.

35. E. L. McGlinchey et al., "The Effect of Sleep Deprivation on Vocal Expression of Emotion in Adolescents and Adults," *Sleep* 34, no. 9 (2011): 1233–41.

36. J. A. Caldwell, J. L. Caldwell, and R. M. Schmidt, "Alertness Management Strategies for Operational Contexts," *Sleep Medicine Reviews* 12, no. 4 (2008): 257–73; M. S. Christian and A. P. J. Ellis, "Examining the Effects of Sleep Deprivation on Workplace Deviance: A Self-Regulatory Perspective," *Academy of Management Journal* 54, no. 5 (2011): 913–34; E. T. Kahn-Greene et al., "Sleep Deprivation Adversely Affects Interpersonal Responses to Frustration," *Personality and Individual Differences* 41, no. 8 (2006): 1433–43; and B. A. Scott and T. A. Judge, "Insomnia, Emotions, and Job Satisfaction: A Multilevel Study," *Journal of Management* 32, no. 5 (2006): 622–45.

37. C. Anderson and D. L. Dickinson, "Bargaining and Trust: The Effects of 36-h Total Sleep Deprivation on Socially Interactive Decisions," *Journal of Sleep Research* 19, no. 1 pt. 1 (2010): 54–63.

38. J. A. Horne, "Human Sleep, Sleep Loss, and Behavior: Implications for the Prefrontal Cortex and Psychiatric Disorder," *British Journal of Psychiatry* 162, no. 3 (1993): 413–19.

39. Christian and Ellis, "Examining the Effects of Sleep Deprivation," 913–34; and C. M. Barnes et al., "Lack of Sleep and Unethical Behavior," *Organizational Behavior and Human Decision Processes* 115, no. 2 (2011): 169–80.

Notes

40. Barnes et al., "Sleepy First Impressions: Lack of Sleep and the Development of Leader-Follower Relationships Over Time" (working paper, Washington University, Seattle, WA, 2015).
41. C. L. Porath, "An Antidote to Incivility," *Harvard Business Review,* April 2016, 101–111.
42. F. Harburg, "Corporate Athlete Course, by the Human Performance Institute Division of Wellness and Prevention," presented at the Conference Board's Chief Environmental, Health & Safety Officers Council, May 16, 2012.
43. S. Phillips, "Mindfulness: An Unexpected Antidote to Workplace Stress," *Healing Together for Couples* (blog), PsychCentral, http://blogs.psychcentral.com/healing-together/2015/08/mindfulness-an-unexpected-antidote-to-workplace-stress/.
44. D. Gelles, "The Mind Business," *Financial Times,* August 24, 2012, http://www.ft.com/cms/s/2/d9cb7940-ebea-11e1-985a-00144feab49a.html.
45. J. Hunter, "Is Mindfulness Good for Business?" *Mindful,* April 2013, 52–59.
46. Gelles, "The Mind Business," http://www.ft.com/cms/s/2/d9cb7940-ebea-11e1-985a-00144feab49a.html.

Chapter 6: The Fundamentals

1. L. Street, "Our Examples of 'Enviable' Workplace Culture," Motley Fool Culture website, January 16, 2015, http://culture.fool.com/category/employee-growth/page/2/.
2. S. B. Sitkin and J. R. Hackman, "Developing Team Leadership: An Interview with Coach Mike Krzyzewski," *Academy of Management Learning and Education* 10, no. 3 (2011): 494–501.
3. Sitkin and Hackman, "Developing Team Leadership."
4. A. J. C. Cuddy, M. Kohut, and J. Neffinger, "Connect, Then Lead: To Exert Influence You Must Balance Competence with Warmth," *Harvard Business Review,* July–August 2013, 2–9.
5. Cuddy, Kohut, and Neffinger, "Connect, Then Lead," 2–9; and A. Cuddy, "In Debates, Watch for Signs of Warmth: Q&A with Amy Cuddy," posted by B. Lillie, TEDBlog, October 1, 2012, http://blog.ted.com/in-debates-watch-for-signs-of-warmth-qa-with-amy-cuddy/.
6. A. J. C. Cuddy, P. Glick, and A. Beninger, "The Dynamics of Warmth and Competence Judgments, and Their Outcomes in Organizations," *Research in Organizational Behavior* 31 (2011): 73–98; and Cuddy, Kohut, and Neffinger, "Connect, Then Lead," 2–9.
7. Sitkin and Hackman, "Developing Team Leadership."

Notes

8. C. Porath, A. Gerbasi, and S. Schorch, "The Effects of Civility on Advice, Leadership, and Performance," *Journal of Applied Psychology* 100, no. 5 (2015): 1527–41.

9. Cuddy, Kohut, and Neffinger, "Connect, Then Lead," 2–9.

10. Cuddy, Kohut, and Neffinger, "Connect, Then Lead," 2–9; and Cuddy, "In Debates, Watch for Signs of Warmth," http://blog.ted.com /in-debates-watch-for-signs-of-warmth-qa-with-amy-cuddy/.

11. A. Todorov, M. Pakrashi, and N. N. Oosterhof, "Evaluating Faces on Trustworthiness After Minimal Time Exposure," *Social Cognition* 27, no. 6 (2009): 813–33.

12. C. Lambert, "The Psyche on Automatic," *Harvard Magazine*, November–December 2010, http://harvardmagazine.com/2010/11/the-psyche-on-auto matic.

13. Cuddy, Kohut, and Neffinger, "Connect, Then Lead," 2–9.

14. R. M. Ryan and E. L. Deci, "Self-Determination Theory and the Facilita-tion of Intrinsic Motivation, Social Development, and Well-Being," *American Psychologist* 55, no. 1 (2000): 68–78; and E. L. Deci, J. P. Connell, and R. M. Ryan, "Self-Determination in a Work Organization," *Journal of Applied Psychology* 74, no. 4 (1989): 580–90.

15. M. Moieni and N. I. Eisenberger, "Neural Correlates of Social Pain," in *Social Neuroscience: Biological Approaches to Social Psychology*, ed. E. Harmon-Jones and M. Inzlicht (forthcoming, 2016); M. L. Meyer, K. D. Williams, and N. I. Eisenberger, "Why Social Pain Can Live On: Different Neural Mechanisms Are Associated with Reliving Social and Physical Pain," *PLoS One* 10, no. 6 (2015): e0128294; N. I. Eisenberger, "Meta-Analytic Evidence for the Role of the Anterior Cingulate Cortex in Social Pain," *Social Cognitive and Affective Neuroscience* 10, no. 1 (2015): 1–2 ; and N. I. Eisenberger, "Social Pain and the Brain: Controversies, Questions, and Where to Go from Here," *Annual Review of Psychology* 66 (2015): 601–29.

16. C. L. Porath, "Civility," in *The Oxford Handbook of Positive Organizational Scholarship*, ed. K. S. Cameron and G. M. Spreitzer (New York: Oxford University Press, 2011), 439–48; and R. M. Tobin et al., "Personality, Emo-tional Experience, and Efforts to Control Emotions," *Journal of Personality and Social Psychology* 79, no. 4 (2000): 656–69.

17. R. Gutman, "The Untapped Power of Smiling," *Forbes*, March 22, 2011, http://www.forbes.com/sites/ericsavitz/2011/03/22/the-untapped-power -of-smiling/.

18. Gutman, "The Untapped Power of Smiling," http://www.forbes.com/sites /ericsavitz/2011/03/22/the-untapped-power-of-smiling/; and "Ron Gutman: The Hidden Power of Smiling," filmed March 2011, TED video, 7:26, http:// www.ted.com/talks/ron_gutman_the_hidden_power_of_smiling.html.

Notes

19. "One Smile Can Make You Feel a Million Dollars," *Scotsman*, March 4, 2005, http://www.scotsman.com/news/one-smile-can-make-you-feel-a-million -dollars-1-738272.
20. E. L. Abel and M. L. Kruger, "Smile Intensity in Photographs Predicts Longevity," *Psychological Science* 21, no. 4 (2010): 542–44.
21. U. Dimberg and S. Söderkvist, "The Voluntary Facial Action Technique: A Method to Test the Facial Feedback Hypothesis," *Journal of Nonverbal Behavior* 35, no. 1 (2011): 17–33.
22. L. Buscaglia. *Love*. (New York: Fawcett Crest, 1972).
23. A. A. Grandey et al., "Is 'Service with a Smile' Enough? Authenticity of Positive Displays During Service Encounters," *Organizational Behavior and Human Decision Processes* 96, no. 1 (2005): 38–55.
24. Gutman, "The Untapped Power of Smiling," http://www.forbes.com/sites /ericsavitz/2011/03/22/the-untapped-power-of-smiling/.
25. Cuddy, Kohut, and Neffinger, "Connect, Then Lead," 2–9; and Cuddy, "In Debates, Watch for Signs of Warmth," http://blog.ted.com /in-debates-watch-for-signs-of-warmth-qa-with-amy-cuddy/.
26. M. Kohut, "Executive Presence: The Inner Game," Medium website, November 23, 2015, https://medium.com/@besmonte/executive-presence -the-inner-game-1f153c9f143d#.e2lan3my9; Cuddy, Kohut, and Neffinger, "Connect, Then Lead," 2–9; and Cuddy, "In Debates, Watch for Signs of Warmth," http://blog.ted.com/in-debates-watch-for-signs-of-warmth-qa-with -amy-cuddy/.
27. Cuddy, "In Debates, Watch for Signs of Warmth," http://blog.ted.com /in-debates-watch-for-signs-of-warmth-qa-with-amy-cuddy/.
28. M. Gladwell, "The Naked Face," *New Yorker*, August 5, 2002, http:// gladwell.com/the-naked-face/.
29. V. I. Sessa and J. J. Taylor, *Executive Selection: Strategies for Success* (San Francisco: Jossey-Bass, 2000).
30. T. Schwartz, "Why Appreciation Matters So Much," *Harvard Business Review* online, January 23, 2012, https://hbr.org/2012/01/why-appreciation-matters -so-mu.html.
31. L. Street, "Coffee Brews Conversation," Motley Fool Culture website, December 3, 2014, http://culture.fool.com/category/employee-growth /page/2/.
32. L. Street, "Foolientation Secrets from a Recruiter," Motley Fool Culture website, July 14, 2015, http://culture.fool.com/2015/07/jobs-foolientation -newhire-employee-orientation-onboarding-hiring/.
33. J. R. Detert and E. R. Burris, "Leadership Behavior and Employee Voice: Is the Door Really Open?" *Academy of Management Journal* 50, no. 4 (2007): 869–84.

34. K. J. Lloyd et al., "Is My Boss Really Listening to Me? The Impact of Perceived Supervisor Listening on Emotional Exhaustion, Turnover Intention, and Organizational Citizenship Behavior," *Journal of Business Ethics* 130, no. 3 (2015): 509–24.
35. S. Shellenbarger, "Tuning In: Improving Your Listening Skills," *Wall Street Journal,* July 22, 2014, http://www.wsj.com/articles/tuning-in-how-to-listen-better-1406070727.
36. Shellenbarger, "Tuning In," http://www.wsj.com/articles/tuning-in-how-to-listen-better-1406070727.
37. Shellenbarger, "Tuning In," http://www.wsj.com/articles/tuning-in-how-to-listen-better-1406070727.
38. Shellenbarger, "Tuning In," http://www.wsj.com/articles/tuning-in-how-to-listen-better-1406070727.
39. Shellenbarger, "Tuning In," http://www.wsj.com/articles/tuning-in-how-to-listen-better-1406070727; and "Julian Treasure: 5 Ways to Listen Better," filmed July 2011, TED video, 7:50, https://www.ted.com/talks/julian_treasure_5_ways_to_listen_better?language=en#t-59584.
40. Cuddy, Kohut, and Neffinger, "Connect, Then Lead," 2–9.

Chapter 7: Judge Not

1. E. Piqué, *Pope Francis: Life and Revolution: A Biography of Jorge Bergoglio* (Chicago: Loyola Press, 2014).
2. Piqué, *Pope Francis: Life and Revolution.*
3. Piqué, *Pope Francis: Life and Revolution*; and R. Gillett, "The Most Influential Leadership Moments We've Seen from Pope Francis So Far," *Business Insider,* September 24, 2015.
4. J. Yardley, "A Humble Pope, Challenging the World," *New York Times,* September 18, 2015, http://nyti.ms/1KxQpIQ; and Piqué, *Pope Francis: Life and Revolution.*
5. Piqué, *Pope Francis: Life and Revolution*; A. Ivereigh, *The Great Reformer: Francis and the Making of a Radical Pope* (New York: Henry Holt, 2014); and Yardley, "A Humble Pope, Challenging the World," http://nyti.ms/1KxQpIQ.
6. Piqué, *Pope Francis: Life and Revolution*; Ivereigh, *The Great Reformer*; and Yardley, "A Humble Pope, Challenging the World," http://nyti.ms/1KxQpIQ.
7. I. San Martin, "Pope Francis Stresses That the Year of Mercy Is Worldwide," *Crux,* December 17, 2015, http://www.cruxnow.com/church/2015/12/17/pope-francis-stresses-that-the-year-of-mercy-is-worldwide/.
8. K. Y. Williams and C. A. O'Reilly, "Demography and Diversity in Organizations: A Review of 40 Years of Research," in *Research in Organizational*

Notes

Behavior, ed. B. Staw and R. Sutton, vol. 20 (Greenwich, CT: JAI Press. 1998), 77–140; and L. Ramarajan and D. Thomas, "A Positive Approach to Studying Diversity in Organizations," in *The Oxford Handbook of Positive Organizational Scholarship,* ed. G. M. Spreitzer and K. S. Cameron (New York: Oxford University Press, 2011), 552–65.

9. S. A. Hewlett, M. Marshall, and L. Sherbin, "How Diversity Can Drive Innovation," *Harvard Business Review,* December 2013, 30, https://hbr.org/2013/12/how-diversity-can-drive-innovation/ar/1.

10. "Two-Thirds of People Consider Diversity Important When Deciding Where to Work, Glassdoor Survey," press release, Glassdoor, November 17, 2014, http://www.glassdoor.com/press/twothirds-people-diversity-important-deciding-work-glassdoor-survey-2.

11. C. Staats, K. Capatosto, R. A. Wright, and D. Contractor. "State of the Science: Implicit Bias Review 2015," Kirwan Institute for the Study of Race and Ethnicity (2015).

12. M. Zimmermann, "Neurophysiology of Sensory Systems," in *Fundamentals of Sensory Physiology,* ed. R. F. Schmidt (Berlin: Springer Berlin Heidelberg, 1986), 68–116.

13. B. Welle, "Google's Unconscious Bias Journey," online video, *Unbiasing* guide, Google re:Work, https://rework.withgoogle.com/guides/unbiasing-raise-awareness/steps/learn-about-googles-unbiasing-journey/.

14. A. J. C. Cuddy, S. T. Fiske, and P. Glick, "The BIAS map: Behaviors from Intergroup Affect and Stereotypes," *Journal of Personality and Social Psychology* 92, no. 4 (2007): 631–48.

15. Ramarajan and Thomas, "A Positive Approach to Studying Diversity in Organizations," 552–65.

16. L. Jampol and V. Zayas, "The Dark Side of White Lies in the Workplace: Women are Given Nicer but Less Accurate Performance Feedback than Men" (working paper, London Business School, London, under review).

17. Jampol and Zayas, "The Dark Side of White Lies."

18. Welle, "Google's Unconscious Bias Journey," https://rework.with google.com/guides/unbiasing-raise-awareness/steps/learn-about-googles-unbiasing-journey/.

19. E. Huet, "Rise of the Bias Busters: How Unconscious Bias Became Silicon Valley's Newest Target," *Forbes,* November 2, 2015, http://www.forbes.com/sites/ellenhuet/2015/11/02/rise-of-the-bias-busters-how-unconscious-bias-became-silicon-valleys-newest-target/#c1dc63a7cb1f.

20. J. J. van Bavel and W. A. Cunningham, "A Social Identity Approach to Person Memory: Group Membership, Collective Identification, and Social Role Shape Attention and Memory," *Personality and Social Psychological Bulletin* 38, no. 12 (2012): 1566–78.

Notes

21. J. van Bavel, "Racial Biases Fade Away Toward Members of Your Own Group," *Research News*, Ohio State University, March 23, 2009, http://researchnews.osu.edu/archive/racebias.htm.

22. M. R. Banaji, M. H. Bazerman, and D. Chugh, "How (Un)ethical Are Your Decisions?" *Harvard Business Review*, December 2003, 56–64.

23. Banaji, Bazerman, and Chugh, "How (Un)ethical Are Your Decisions?" 56–64.

24. T. Clark and W. McGarvey, "Guest Commentary: Coming Together to Denounce Both Terror and Discrimination Against Muslims," Opinion, *East Bay Times* (Bay Area News Group), January 1, 2016, http://www.eastbaytimes.com/opinion/ci_29326586/guest-commentary-coming-together-denounce-both-terror-and.

25. J. P. Wanous and M. A. Youtz, "Solution Diversity and the Quality of Group Decisions," *Academy of Management Journal* 29, no. 1 (1986): 149–59.

26. Google was involved with the release of this information.

27. Welle, "Google's Unconscious Bias Journey," https://rework.with google.com/guides/unbiasing-raise-awareness/steps/learn-about-googles-unbiasing-journey/.

28. Welle, "Google's Unconscious Bias Journey," https://rework.with google.com/guides/unbiasing-raise-awareness/steps/learn-about-googles-unbiasing-journey/.

29. A. W. Brooks et al., "Investors Prefer Entrepreneurial Ventures Pitched by Attractive Men," *Proceedings of the National Academy of Sciences* 111, no. 12 (2014): 4427–31.

30. Welle, "Google's Unconscious Bias Journey," https://rework.with google.com/guides/unbiasing-raise-awareness/steps/learn-about-googles-unbiasing-journey/.

31. R. F. Martell, D. M. Lane, and C. Emrich, "Male–Female Differences: A Computer Simulation," *American Psychologist* 51, no. 2 (1996): 157–59.

32. Welle, "Google's Unconscious Bias Journey," https://rework.withgoogle.com/guides/unbiasing-raise-awareness/steps/learn-about-googles-unbiasing-journey/.

33. Welle, "Google's Unconscious Bias Journey," https://rework.withgoogle.com/guides/unbiasing-raise-awareness/steps/learn-about-googles-unbiasing-journey/.

34. B. Welle, "Unconscious Bias @ Work," online video, *Unbiasing* guide, Google re:Work, https://rework.withgoogle.com/guides/unbiasing-raise-awareness/steps/watch-unconscious-bias-at-work/.

35. "Learn About Google's Workshop Experiment," *Unbiasing* guide, Google re:Work, https://rework.withgoogle.com/guides/unbiasing-raise-awareness/steps/learn-about-Googles-workshop-experiment/.

Notes

36. Welle, "Google's Unconscious Bias Journey," https://rework.with google.com/guides/unbiasing-raise-awareness/steps/learn-about-googles -unbiasing-journey/.
37. "Tool: Use Unbiasing Checklists," *Unbiasing* guide, Google re:Work, https:// rework.withgoogle.com/guides/unbiasing-use-structure-and-criteria/ steps/use-unbiasing-checklists/.
38. "Tool: Use Unbiasing Checklists," https://rework.withgoogle.com/ guides/unbiasing-use-structure-and-criteria/steps/use-unbiasing -checklists/.

Chapter 8: Give More

1. A. M. Grant, *Give and Take: A Revolutionary Approach to Success* (New York: Viking Press, 2013).
2. Grant, *Give and Take*.
3. C. Porath et al., "How Giving Meaning to Others Fuels Performance at Work" (working paper, Georgetown University, Washington, DC, 2016).
4. R. Cross, R. Rebele, and A. Grant, "Collaborative Overload," *Harvard Business Review*, January–February 2016.
5. Cross, Rebele, and Grant, "Collaborative Overload."
6. Cross, Rebele, and Grant, "Collaborative Overload."
7. Cross, Rebele, and Grant, "Collaborative Overload."
8. Cross, Rebele, and Grant, "Collaborative Overload."
9. Warren Bennis, meeting with author, July 31, 2012.
10. B. P. Owens, M. D. Johnson, and T. R. Mitchell, "Expressed Humility in Organizations: Implications for Performance, Teams, and Leadership," *Organization Science* 24, no. 5 (2013): 1517–38.
11. Owens, Johnson, and Mitchell, "Expressed Humility in Organizations," 1517–38.
12. H. Zhang, *How Do I Recognize Thee, Let Me Count the Ways* (Thought Leadership Whitepaper, IBM Smarter Workforce Institute, 2015), http:// www-01.ibm.com/common/ssi/cgi-bin/ssialias?subtype=WH&infotype =SA&htmlfid=LOW14298USEN&attachment=LOW14298USEN.PDF.
13. T. Amabile and S. Kramer, *The Progress Principle: Using Small Wins to Ignite Joy, Engagement, and Creativity at Work* (Boston: Harvard Business Review Press, 2011).
14. W. Baker, "Openbook Finance at Zingerman's," GlobaLens Case 1-429-091, October 2010.
15. Baker, "Openbook Finance at Zingerman's."
16. T. Schwartz, J. Gomes, and C. McCarthy, *Be Excellent at Anything: The Four Keys to Transforming the Way We Work and Live* (New York: Free Press, 2010).

17. J. A. Smith, "Five Ways to Cultivate Gratitude at Work," Greater Good Science Center, University of California, Berkeley, May 16, 2013, http://greatergood.berkeley.edu/article/item/five_ways_to_cultivate_gratitude _at_work; and J. Kaplan, "The Gratitude Survey," produced by Penn Schoen Berland for the John Templeton Foundation, June–October 2012.

18. A. M. Grant and F. Gino, "A Little Thanks Goes a Long Way: Explaining Why Gratitude Expressions Motivate Prosocial Behavior," *Journal of Personality and Social Psychology* 98, no. 6 (2010): 946–55.

19. Grant and Gino, "A Little Thanks Goes a Long Way," 946–55; and A. Grant, "How to Succeed Professionally by Helping Others," *Atlantic*, March 17, 2014, http://www.theatlantic.com/health/archive/2014/03/how-to-succeed -professionally-by-helping-others/284429/.

20. S. Lyubomirsky, K. M. Sheldon, and D. Schkade, "Pursuing Happiness: The Architecture of Sustainable Change," *Review of General Psychology* 9, no. 2 (2005): 111–31; M. E. McCullough, J.-A. Tsang, and R. A. Emmons, "Gratitude in Intermediate Affective Terrain: Links of Grateful Moods to Individual Differences and Daily Emotional Experience," *Journal of Personality and Social Psychology* 86, no. 2 (2004): 295–309; R. A. Emmons and M. E. McCullough, "Counting Blessings Versus Burdens: An Experimental Investigation of Gratitude and Subjective Well-Being in Daily Life," *Journal of Personality and Social Psychology* 84, no. 2 (2003): 377–89; M. E. Seligman et al., "Positive Psychology Progress: Empirical Validation of Interventions," *American Psychologist* 60, no. 5 (2005): 410–21; and R. A. Emmons and M. E. McCullough, ed., *The Psychology of Gratitude* (New York: Oxford University Press, 2004).

21. Kaplan, "The Gratitude Survey."

22. R. Emmons, "How Gratitude Can Help You Through Hard Times," Greater Good Science Center, University of California, Berkeley, May 13, 2013, http://greatergood.berkeley.edu/article/item/how_gratitude_can_help_you _through_hard_times; and McCullough, Tsang, and Emmons, "Gratitude in Intermediate Affective Terrain," 295–309; Emmons and McCullough, "Counting Blessings Versus Burdens," 377–89; and Emmons and McCullough, *The Psychology of Gratitude*.

23. G. Spreitzer and C. Porath, "Creating Sustainable Performance: Four Ways to Help Your Employees—and Organization—Thrive," *Harvard Business Review*, January–February 2012, 92–99; G. Spreitzer and C. Porath, "Enabling Thriving at Work," in *How to Be a Positive Leader: Small Actions, Big Impact*, ed. J. E. Dutton and G. M. Spreitzer (San Francisco: Berrett-Koehler, 2014), 45–54; and Baker, "Openbook Finance at Zingerman's."

24. Spreitzer and Porath, "Creating Sustainable Performance," 92–99.

Notes

25. M. Losada, "The Complex Dynamics of High Performance Teams," *Mathematical and Computer Modelling* 30, nos. 9–10 (1999): 179–192; and M. Losada and E. Heaphy, "The Role of Positivity and Connectivity in the Performance of Business Teams: A Nonlinear Dynamics Model," *American Behavioral Scientist* 47, no. 6 (2004): 740–65.

26. Gallup, *State of the American Workplace: Employee Engagement Insights for U.S. Business Leaders* (Lincoln, NE: Gallup, 2012).

27. D. Goleman and R. E. Boyatzis, "Social Intelligence and the Biology of Leadership," *Harvard Business Review*, September 2008.

28. Goleman and Boyatzis, "Social Intelligence and the Biology of Leadership."

29. C. Niessen, S. Sonnentag, and F. Sach, "Thriving at Work—A Diary Study," *Journal of Organizational Behavior* 33, no. 4 (2012): 468–87.

30. D. R. May, R. L. Gilson, and L. M. Harter, "The Psychological Conditions of Meaningfulness, Safety, and Availability and the Engagement of the Human Spirit at Work," *Journal of Occupational and Organizational Psychology* 77, no. 1 (2004): 11–37.

31. C. Leufstadius et al., "Meaningfulness in Daily Occupations Among Individuals with Persistent Mental Illness," *Journal of Occupational Science* 15, no. 1 (2008): 27–35; G. M. Spreitzer, M. A. Kizilos, and S. W. Nason, "A Dimensional Analysis of the Relationship Between Psychological Empowerment and Effectiveness, Satisfaction, and Strain," *Journal of Management* 23, no. 5 (1997): 679–704; and P. E. McKnight and T. B. Kashdan, "Purpose in Life as a System That Creates and Sustains Health and Well-Being: An Integrative, Testable Theory," *Review of General Psychology* 13, no. 3 (2009): 242–51.

32. C. Porath et al., "How Giving Meaning to Others Fuels Performance at Work" (working paper, Georgetown University, Washington, DC, 2016).

33. A. M. Grant, "How Customers Can Rally Your Troops: End Users Can Energize Your Workforce Far Better than Your Managers Can," *Harvard Business Review*, June 2011, 97–103; and A. M. Grant, "Outsourcing Inspiration," in *How to Be a Positive Leader: Small Actions, Big Impact*, ed. J. E. Dutton and G. M. Spreitzer (San Francisco: Berrett-Koehler, 2014), 22–31.

34. "Our Mission," My Saint My Hero website, https://mysaintmyhero.com/our-mission/.

35. "Our Mission: Helping the World Invest—Better," Motley Fool website, http://www.fool.com/press/about-the-motley-fool.aspx.

36. D. Conant and M. Norgaard, *TouchPoints: Creating Powerful Leadership Connections in the Smallest of Moments* (San Francisco: Jossey-Bass, 2011); and D. Conant, https://www.bigspeak.com/speakers/douglas-conant/.

37. Conant and Norgaard, *TouchPoints*; and D. Conant, https://www.bigspeak.com/speakers/douglas-conant/.

38. Conant and Norgaard, *TouchPoints*; and D. Conant, https://www.bigspeak
    .com/speakers/douglas-conant/.

39. Conant and Norgaard, *TouchPoints*; and D. Conant, https://www.bigspeak
    .com/speakers/douglas-conant/.

40. Conant and Norgaard, *TouchPoints*; and D. Conant, https://www.bigspeak
    .com/speakers/douglas-conant/.

41. Conant and Norgaard, *TouchPoints*; and D. R. Conant, "Secrets of Positive
    Feedback," *Harvard Business Review* online, February 16, 2011, https://hbr
    .org/2011/02/secrets-of-positive-feedback/.

Chapter 9: Practice E-civility

1. E. Wong, "A Stinging Office Memo Boomerangs; Chief Executive Is Criti-
   cized After Upbraiding Workers by E-Mail," *Business Day, New York Times*,
   April 5, 2001, http://www.nytimes.com/2001/04/05/business/stinging
   -office-memo-boomerangs-chief-executive-criticized-after-upbraiding
   .html?pagewanted=all; and "Cerner Example," *BizCom in the News* (blog),
   http://www.bizcominthenews.com/files/cerner-1.pdf.

2. H. Osman, *Don't Reply All: 18 Email Tactics That Help You Write Better
   Emails and Improve Communication with Your Team*, Kindle Locations
   152–155 (published by author, 2015); and D. Shipley and W. Schwalbe,
   Send: Why People Email So Badly and How to Do It Better (New York: Alfred
   A. Knopf, 2010).

3. A. Grant, "6 Ways to Get Me to Email You Back," Pulse post, LinkedIn,
   June 24, 2013.

4. Grant, "6 Ways to Get Me to Email You Back."

5. T. Weiss, "You've Got Mail: You're Fired," *Forbes*, August, 31, 2006, http://
   www.forbes.com/2006/08/31/leadership-radio-shack-management-cx
   _tw_0831layoffs.html.

6. C. L. Porath, "No Time to Be Nice at Work," *Sunday Review, New York
   Times*, June 19, 2015, http://www.nytimes.com/2015/06/21/opinion
   /sunday/is-your-boss-mean.html?_r=0.

7. F. Kooti et al., "Evolution of Conversations in the Age of Email Overload,"
   International World Wide Web Conference Committee, May 18–22,
   2015, Florence, Italy. http://www-scf.usc.edu/~kooti/files/kooti_email
   .pdf; and J. Beck, "How Quickly Will Your Email Get A Response?,"
   The Atlantic, October 7, 2015. http://www.theatlantic.com/technology
   /archive/2015/10/how-quickly-will-your-email-get-a-response/409429/.

8. L. Evans, "You Aren't Imagining It: Email Is Making You More Stressed
   Out," *Fast Company*, September 24, 2014, http://www.fastcompany.com
   /3036061/the-future-of-work/you-arent-imagining-it-email-is-making-you
   -more-stressed-out.

9. Evans, "You Aren't Imagining It," http://www.fastcompany.com/3036061/the-future-of-work/you-arent-imagining-it-email-is-making-you-more-stressed-out.

10. K. Kushlev and E. W. Dunn, "Checking Email Less Frequently Reduces Stress," *Computers in Human Behavior* 43 (2015): 220–28.

11. *Civility in America 2014*, survey, conducted by Weber Shandwick, Powell Tate, and KRC Research, http://www.webershandwick.com/uploads/news/files/civility-in-america-2014.pdf.

12. J. Lin, "Doing Something About the 'Impossible Problem' of Abuse in Online Games," *Re/code*, July 7, 2015, http://on.recode.net/1G3iUHt.; and B. Maher, "Can a Video Game Company Tame Toxic Behavior?," *Nature*, March 30, 2016.

13. Lin, "Doing Something About the 'Impossible Problem,'" http://on.recode.net/1G3iUHt.

14. B. Maher, "Can a Video Game Company Tame Toxic Behavior?," *Nature*, March 30, 2016.

15. Maher, "Can a Video Game Company Tame Toxic Behavior?," *Nature*, March 30, 2016.

16. Lin, "Doing Something About the 'Impossible Problem,'" http://on.recode.net/1G3iUHt.

17. Lin, "Doing Something About the 'Impossible Problem,'" http://on.recode.net/1G3iUHt.

18. Maher, "Can a Video Game Company Tame Toxic Behavior?," *Nature*, March 30, 2016.

19. Lin, "Doing Something About the 'Impossible Problem,'" http://on.recode.net/1G3iUHt.

20. Lin, "Doing Something About the 'Impossible Problem,'" http://on.recode.net/1G3iUHt.

21. Lin, "Doing Something About the 'Impossible Problem,'" http://on.recode.net/1G3iUHt.

22. Maher, "Can a Video Game Company Tame Toxic Behavior?," *Nature*, March 30, 2016.

Chapter 10: Recruit

1. J. Wooden and S. Jamison, *Wooden on Leadership* (New York: McGraw-Hill, 2005).

2. Wooden and Jamison, *Wooden on Leadership*.

3. "Leadership Lessons from UCLA's John Wooden," *Business Week*, May 20, 2009, http://www.businessweek.com/managing/content/may2009/ca20090520_806471.htm.

4. Wooden and Jamison, *Wooden on Leadership*.

Notes

5. Wooden and Jamison, *Wooden on Leadership*.
6. M. Housman, and D. Minor, "Toxic Workers," (working paper 16-057, Harvard University, Boston, MA, 2015), http://www.hbs.edu /faculty/Publication%20Files/16-057_d45c0b4f-fa19-49de-8f1b -4b12fe054fea.pdf.; and D. Minor, "Just How Toxic Are Toxic Employees?" *The Water Cooler* (blog), Google, re:Work, January 20, 2016, https://rework.withgoogle.com/blog/how-toxic-are-toxic-employees/; and N. Tores, "It's Better to Avoid a Toxic Employee than Hire a Superstar," *Harvard Business Review* online, December 9, 2015, https://hbr .org/2015/12/its-better-to-avoid-a-toxic-employee-than-hire-a-superstar.
7. C. Porath and A. Gerbasi, "Does Civility Pay?" *Organizational Dynamics* 44, no. 4 (2015): 281–86, http://www.sciencedirect.com/science/article /pii/S0090261615000595; and A. Parker, A. Gerbasi, and C. L. Porath, "The Effects of De-Energizing Ties in Organizations and How to Manage Them," *Organizational Dynamics* 42, no. 2 (2013): 110–18.
8. T. Macan, "The Employment Interview: A Review of Current Studies and Directions for Future Research," *Human Resource Management Review* 19 (2009): 203–18, http://mavweb.mnsu.edu/howard/The%20employment %20interview.pdf.
9. B. Taylor, "Why Amazon Is Copying Zappos and Paying Employees to Quit," *Harvard Business Review* online, April 14, 2014, https://hbr.org/2014/04 /why-amazon-is-copying-zappos-and-paying-employees-to-quit/.
10. Jay Moldenhauer-Salazar, telephone interview with author, May 26, 2016; and "Riot Games: Assessing Toxicity in the Work Environment," Google re:Work, https://rework.withgoogle.com/case-studies/riot-games -assessing-toxicity/.
11. Jay Moldenhauer-Salazar, telephone interview with author, May 26, 2016; and "Riot Games: Assessing Toxicity in the Work Environment," Google re:Work, https://rework.withgoogle.com/case-studies/riot-games -assessing-toxicity/.
12. Jay Moldenhauer-Salazar, telephone interview with author, May 26, 2016; and "Riot Games: Assessing Toxicity in the Work Environment," Google re:Work, https://rework.withgoogle.com/case-studies/riot-games -assessing-toxicity/.
13. S. Davis, *Wooden: A Coach's Life* (New York: Time Books / Henry Holt, 2014).
14. "Make Interviewing Everyone's Job," *Hiring* guide, Google re:Work, https://rework.withgoogle.com/guides/hiring-train-your-interviewers /steps/make-interviewing-everyones-job/.
15. A. Deutschman, "Inside the Mind of Jeff Bezos," *Fast Company*, August 1, 2004, http://www.fastcompany.com/50661/inside-mind-jeff-bezos.

Notes

Chapter 11: Coach

1. Davis, *Wooden: A Coach's Life.*; and Wooden and Jamison, *Wooden on Leadership.*
2. Southwest Airlines website, https://www.southwest.com/html/about -southwest/index.html?int=.
3. Dignity Health website, http://www.dignityhealth.org/cm/content/pages /history-and-mission.asp.
4. Starbucks website, http://www.starbucks.com/about-us/company-informa tion/mission-statement.
5. Starbucks website, http://www.starbucks.com/about-us/company-informa tion/mission-statement.
6. A. Roenigk, "Lotus pose on two," *ESPN*, August 21, 2013, http://espn.go.com /nfl/story/_/id/9581925/seattle-seahawks-use-unusual-techniques-practice -espn-magazine.
7. Roenigk, "Lotus pose on two," *ESPN*.
8. M. Moriarty, "Coach Pete Carroll's No.1 rule makes sense in the workplace, too," *Pudget Sound Business Journal*, August 4, 2014, http://www .bizjournals.com/seattle/blog/2014/07/coach-pete-carrolls-no-1-rule -makes-sense-in-the.html.
9. I say this even though I am aware of discriminatory lawsuits against Chick-fil-A. Information on this history of this can be found at: http:// www.forbes.com/forbes/2007/0723/080.html and http://www.examiner .com/article/report-chick-fil-a-sued-19-times-for-discriminating -against-minority-groups. Information on some related settlements can be found at http://www.businessinsurance.com/article/20140606/NEWS07 /140609862.
10. M. A. Vu, "Chick-fil-A CEO: Jesus Teachings Helped Increase Sales," *Christian Post*, April 17, 2011, http://www.christianpost.com/news /chick-fil-a-ceo-jesus-teachings-helped-increase-sales-49867/.
11. T. Starnes, "Chick-fil-A Gives Free Food to Motorists Stranded in Southern Snowstorm," Opinion, FoxNews.com, January 29, 2014, http://www .foxnews.com/opinion/2014/01/29/chick-fil-gives-free-food-to-motorists -stranded-in-southern-snowstorm.html.
12. S. Clarke, "A Franchisee Gives Needy Man Free Meal, His Own Gloves," ABC News online, January 13, 2015, http://abcnews.go.com /US/chick-fil-franchisee-needy-man-free-meal-gloves/story?id=28182111.
13. J. Guynes, "Chick-fil-A Delivers Food on Sunday to Tornado Responders and Victims," *Insider* (blog), FoxNews.com, December 28, 2015, http:// insider.foxnews.com/2015/12/28/chick-fil-broke-its-closed-sundays-rule -help-after-texas-tornado.
14. "Accolades," Chick-fil-A website, http://inside.chick-fil-a.com/accolades/.

Notes

15. S. B. Sitkin and J. R. Hackman, "Developing Team Leadership: An Interview with Coach Mike Krzyzewski," *Academy of Management Learning and Education* 10, no. 3 (2011): 494–501.

16. K. Haman, "'One Firm' Approach Treats Colleagues Like Clients," *Orange County Business Journal*, July 27, 2015; and "2015 Best Places to Work in Orange County," *Best Places to Work,* http://bestplacestoworkoc.com/index.php?option=com_content&task=view&id=65.

17. C. L. Porath and C. M. Pearson, 2010. "The Cost of Bad Behavior." *Organizational Dynamics,* 39 (2010): 64–71.

18. Tim Tassopoulos, telephone interview with author, March 3, 2016.

19. G. Spreitzer and C. Porath, "Creating Sustainable Performance," *Harvard Business Review*, 90 (1-2) (2012): 92-99.

Chapter 12: Score

1. C. Pearson and C. Porath, *The Cost of Bad Behavior: How Incivility Is Damaging Your Business and What to Do About It* (New York: Portfolio / Penguin Group, 2009).

2. L. Bock, *Work Rules: Insights from Inside Google That Will Transform How You Live and Lead* (New York: Twelve, 2015).

3. J. Wooden and S. Jamison, *Wooden on Leadership* (New York: McGraw-Hill, 2005).

4. G. Hamel with S. Spence, "Innovation Democracy: W. L. Gore's Original Management Model," Management Innovation eXchange website, September 23, 2010, http://www.managementexchange.com/story/innovation-democracy-wl-gores-original-management-model.

5. Hamel with Spence, "Innovation Democracy."

6. "Teri Kelly and Panel," YouTube video, filmed at the Center for Effective Organizations' Corporate Stewardship Conference at the University of Southern California, Los Angeles, CA, February 20, 2014, 1:26:11, posted by Ctr4EffectiveOrgs March 17, 2014, https://www.youtube.com/watch?v=YCtyFlRCxZ8&feature=youtube.

7. Hamel with Spence, "Innovation Democracy"; and G. Hamel, "W. L. Gore: Lessons from a Management Revolutionary, Part 2," *Gary Hamel's Management 2.0* (blog), *Wall Street Journal*, April, 2, 2010, http://blogs.wsj.com/management/2010/04/02/wl-gore-lessons-from-a-management-revolutionary-part-2/.

8. Hamel, "W. L. Gore, Part 2," http://blogs.wsj.com/management/2010/04/02/wl-gore-lessons-from-a-management-revolutionary-part-2/.

9. "McIntire Professor and Renowned Networks Expert Rob Cross Discusses 'Collaborative Overload' Work Featured on Cover of Harvard Business

Review," University of Virginia McIntire School of Commerce website, January 8, 2016.

10. R. Cross, R. Rebele, and A. Grant, "Collaborative Overload," *Harvard Business Review*, January–February 2016.

11. N. Li et al., "Achieving More with Less: Extra Milers' Behavioral Influences in Teams," *Journal of Applied Psychology* 100, no. 4 (2015): 1025–39.

12. Cross, Rebele, and Grant, "Collaborative Overload."

13. "McIntire Professor and Renowned Networks Expert Rob Cross Discusses 'Collaborative Overload' Work Featured on Cover of Harvard Business Review," University of Virginia McIntire School of Commerce website, January 8, 2016.

14. Cross, Rebele, and Grant, "Collaborative Overload."

15. A. Parker, A. Gerbasi, and C. L. Porath, "The Effects of De-Energizing Ties in Organizations and How to Manage Them," *Organizational Dynamics* 42, no. 2 (2013): 110–18; and A. Gerbasi et al., "Destructive De-Energizing Relationships: How Thriving Buffers Their Effect on Performance," *Journal of Applied Psychology* 100, no. 5 (2015): 1423–33.

16. Parker, Gerbasi, and Porath, "The Effects of De-Energizing Ties in Organizations," 110–18.

17. Parker, Gerbasi, and Porath, "The Effects of De-Energizing Ties in Organizations," 110–18.

18. Parker, Gerbasi, and Porath, "The Effects of De-Energizing Ties in Organizations," 110–18.

19. Parker, Gerbasi, and Porath, "The Effects of De-Energizing Ties in Organizations," 110–18.

20. A. Bryant, "Google's Quest to Build a Better Boss," Business Day, *New York Times*, March 12, 2011, http://www.nytimes.com/2011/03/13/business/13hire.html.

21. Bock, *Work Rules*.

22. Bock, *Work Rules*.

23. L. Street, "Rewarding Your Employees: Try This New Method," Motley Fool Culture website, July 21, 2014, http://culture.fool.com/2014/07/employee-engagement-rewards/.

Chapter 13: Practice

1. "The Wizard's Wisdom: 'Woodenisms,'" *ESPN*, June 4, 2010, http://espn.go.com/mens-college-basketball/news/story?id=5249709.

2. M. Goldsmith and M. Reiter, *Triggers: Creating Behavior That Lasts—Becoming the Person You Want to Be* (New York: Crown Business, 2015).

3. M. Goldsmith with M. Reiter, *What Got You Here Won't Get You There* (New York: Hyperion, 2007), 29.

Notes

4. R. B. Cialdini, *Influence: The Psychology of Persuasion, Revised Edition* (New York: Harper Business, 2006).
5. Goldsmith with Reiter, *What Got You Here Won't Get You There*.
6. Goldsmith with Reiter, *What Got You Here Won't Get You There*.
7. Goldsmith with Reiter, *What Got You Here Won't Get You There*.
8. Goldsmith with Reiter, *What Got You Here Won't Get You There*.
9. T. Amabile and S. Kramer, *The Progress Principle: Using Small Wins to Ignite Joy, Engagement, and Creativity at Work* (Boston: Harvard Business Review Press, 2011).
10. Goldsmith with Reiter, *What Got You Here Won't Get You There*.
11. D. Meyer, *Setting the Table: The Transforming Power of Hospitality in Business* (New York: HarperCollins, 2007).
12. R. I. Sutton, *Good Boss, Bad Boss: How to Be the Best... and Learn from the Worst* (New York: Business Plus, 2010).
13. J. I. Jenkins, "Persuasion as the Cure for Incivility," Commentary, *Wall Street Journal*, January 8, 2013, http://online.wsj.com/news/articles/SB100 01424127887323339704578173860563117812.

Chapter 14: Your Antidote to Incivility

1. A. Caspi et al., "Influence of Life Stress on Depression: Moderation by a Polymorphism in the 5-HTT Gene," *Science* 301, no. 5621 (2003): 386–89.
2. Caspi et al., "Influence of Life Stress on Depression," 386–89.
3. C. Pearson and C. Porath, *The Cost of Bad Behavior: How Incivility Is Damaging Your Business and What to Do About It* (New York: Portfolio / Penguin Group, 2009).
4. M. E. P. Seligman, *Helplessness: On Depression, Development, and Death* (San Francisco: W. H. Freeman, 1975); D. S. Hiroto, "Locus of Control and Learned Helplessness," *Journal of Experimental Psychology* 102, no. 2 (1974): 187–93; D. S. Hiroto and M. E. Seligman, "Generality of Learned Helplessness in Man," *Journal of Personality and Social Psychology* 31, no. 2 (1975): 311–27; and L. A. Engberg et al., "Acquisition of Key-Pecking via Autoshaping as a Function of Prior Experience: 'Learned Laziness?'" *Science* 178, no. 4064 (1972): 1002–4.
5. R. J. Davidson and S. Begley, *The Emotional Life of Your Brain: How Its Unique Patterns Affect the Way You Think, Feel, and Live—and How You Can Change Them* (New York: Hudson Street Press, 2012).
6. Davidson and Begley, *The Emotional Life of Your Brain*.
7. Davidson and Begley, *The Emotional Life of Your Brain*.
8. Davidson and Begley, *The Emotional Life of Your Brain*.
9. G. Spreitzer and C. L. Porath, "Creating Sustainable Performance: Four Ways to Help Your Employees—and Organization—Thrive," *Harvard Business Review*, January–February 2012, 92–99.

Notes

10. C. L. Porath, "An Antidote to Incivility," *Harvard Business Review*, April 2016, 108–111.
11. Porath, "An Antidote to Incivility."
12. S. Lyubomirsky, K. M. Sheldon, and D. Schkade, "Pursuing Happiness: The Architecture of Sustainable Change," *Review of General Psychology* 9, no. 2 (2005): 111–31; and M. Seligman, *Flourish: A Visionary New Understanding of Happiness and Well-Being* (New York: Atria Books, 2012).
13. Porath, "An Antidote to Incivility."
14. T. Amabile and S. Kramer, *The Progress Principle: Using Small Wins to Ignite Joy, Engagement, and Creativity at Work* (Boston: Harvard Business Review Press, 2011).
15. Porath, "An Antidote to Incivility."
16. Porath, "An Antidote to Incivility."
17. S. Toker and M. Biron, "Job Burnout and Depression: Unraveling Their Temporal Relationship and Considering the Role of Physical Activity," *Journal of Applied Psychology* 97, no. 3 (2012): 699–710.
18. L. Blue, "Is Exercise the Best Drug for Depression?" *Time*, June 19, 2010, http://content.time.com/time/health/article/0,8599,1998021,00.html.
19. C. L. Porath, "Civility" (working paper, Georgetown University, Washington, DC, 2016).
20. Center for Positive Organizations, "Job Crafting Exercise," online video, 1:32, Ross School of Business, University of Michigan, http://positiveorgs.bus.umich.edu/cpo-tools/job-crafting-exercise/.
21. A. Wrzesniewski, "Engage in Job Crafting," in *How to Be a Positive Leader: Small Actions, Big Impact*, ed. J. E. Dutton and G. M. Spreitzer (San Francisco: Berrett-Koehler, 2014), 11–21.
22. A. Parker, A. Gerbasi, and C. L. Porath, "The Effects of De-Energizing Ties in Organizations and How to Manage Them," *Organizational Dynamics* 42, no. 2 (2013): 110–18.
23. Porath, "An Antidote to Incivility."

Conclusion

1. "Jordan Spieth Captures Green Jacket," ESPN video, 4:20, posted July 6, 2015, http://espn.go.com/video/clip?id=12676338.
2. "Jordan Spieth Captures Green Jacket," http://espn.go.com/video/clip?id=12676338.
3. N. Gulbis, "The Bond Between Players and Caddies Unlike Anything Else in Golf, or Life," *Golf,* March 10, 2016, http://www.golf.com/tour-and-news/natalie-gulbis-bond-between-players-caddies-unlike-anything-else-golf.

Notes

4. S. Petite, "Even in Defeat, Jordan Spieth Wins," *HuffPost Sports*, July 21, 2015, http://www.huffingtonpost.com/steven-petite/even-in-defeat-jordan -spi_b_7845210.html.
5. K. Van Valkenburg, "Jordan Spieth Gracious in Defeat at PGA," ESPN online, August 17, 2015, http://espn.go.com/golf/pgachampionship15/story/_ /id/13444877/jordan-spieth-gracious-defeat-jason-day-pga-championship.
6. T. Dahlberg, "Column: A Special Win for a Special Player at the Masters," *WTOP*, April 12, 2015 http://wtop.com/golf/2015/04/column-a-special -win-for-a-special-player-at-the-masters/.

Recommended Resources

To Make Work Better

Google's re:Work website: https://g.co/rework

To Combat Unconscious Bias

"How Employees and Managers Can Combat Unconscious Bias" by Veronica Gilrane, *The Water Cooler* blog, Google re:Work, https://rework.withgoogle.com/blog/employees-and-managers-can-combat-unconscious-bias/

To Estimate the Costs of Incivility

The Cost of Bad Behavior: How Incivility Is Damaging Your Business and What to Do About It by Christine Pearson and Christine Porath (New York: Portfolio / Penguin Group, 2009)—see chapter 3 in particular

To Coach Yourself or Others, or Work on Improving Any Behavior

Triggers: Creating Behavior That Lasts—Becoming the Person You Want to Be by Marshall Goldsmith and Mark Reiter (New York: Crown Business, 2015)

What Got You Here Won't Get You There: How Successful People Become Even More Successful by Marshall Goldsmith with Mark Reiter (New York: Hyperion, 2007)

To Manage Energy Effectively

The websites of the Human Performance Institute (https://www.jjhpi.com/) and the Energy Project (http://theenergyproject.com/)

Thrive: The Third Metric to Redefining Success and Creating a Life of Well-Being, Wisdom, and Wonder by Arianna Huffington (New York: Harmony / Crown, 2015)

Rhythm of Life: Living Every Day with Passion and Purpose by Matthew Kelly (Boston: Beacon, 2015)

Recommended Resources

The Power of Full Engagement: Managing Energy, Not Time, Is the Key to High Performance and Personal Renewal by Jim Loehr and Tony Schwartz (New York: Free Press, 2003)

Eat, Move, Sleep: How Small Choices Lead to Big Changes by Tom Rath (New York: Perseus, 2013)

To Create a Culture of Giving

Give and Take: A Revolutionary Approach to Success by Adam Grant (New York: Viking Press, 2013)

To Receive Feedback Better

Thanks for the Feedback: The Science and Art of Receiving Feedback Well by Douglas Stone and Sheila Heen (New York: Viking, 2014)

To Handle Difficult Conversations Well

Difficult Conversations: How to Discuss What Matters Most by Douglas Stone, Bruce Patton, and Sheila Heen, with Roger Fisher (New York: Penguin, 2010)

To Practice E-civility

Don't Reply All: 18 E-mail Tactics That Help You Write Better Emails and Improve Communication with Your Team by Hassan Osman, Kindle Locations 152–155 (Published by author, 2015)

Send: Why People Email So Badly and How to Do It Better by David Shipley and Will Schwalbe (New York: Alfred A. Knopf, 2010)

To Manage Stress or Overload

CrazyBusy by Edward Hallowell (New York: Ballantine, 2006)

To Seek Feedback

The Reflected Best Self Exercise (RBSE), available at the Center for Positive Organizations, Ross School of Business, University of Michigan, http://positiveorgs.bus.umich.edu/cpo-tools/reflected-best-self-exercise-2nd-edition/

To Make Your Job More Fulfilling

The Job Crafting Exercise, available at the Center for Positive Organizations, Ross School of Business, University of Michigan, http://positiveorgs.bus.umich.edu/cpo-tools/job-crafting-exercise/

Recommended Resources

Additional Resources

Work Rules: Insights from Inside Google That Will Transform How You Live and Lead by Laszlo Bock (New York: Twelve, 2015)

The Virgin Way: Everything I Know About Leadership by Richard Branson (New York: Portfolio, 2014)

How to Be a Positive Leader: Small Actions, Big Impact edited by Jane Dutton and Gretchen Spreitzer (San Francisco: Berrett-Koehler, 2014)

Choosing Civility: The Twenty-Five Rules of Considerate Conduct by P. M. Forni (New York: St. Martin's, 2002)

The Civility Solution: What to Do When People Are Rude by P. M. Forni (New York: St. Martin's, 2008)

Shine: Using Brain Science to Get the Best from Your People by Edward Hallowell (Boston: Harvard Business Review Press, 2011)

Love 'Em or Lose 'Em: Getting Good People to Stay by Beverly Kaye and Sharon Jordan-Evans (San Francisco: Berrett-Koehler, 2014)

Encouraging the Heart: A Leader's Guide to Rewarding and Recognizing Others by James Kouzes and Barry Posner (San Francisco: Jossey-Bass, 1999)

Drive: The Surprising Truth About What Motivates Us by Daniel Pink (New York: Riverhead Books, 2009)

Humble Inquiry: The Gentle Art of Asking Instead of Telling by Edgar Schein (San Francisco: Berrett-Koehler, 2013)

Good Boss, Bad Boss: How to Be the Best... and Learn from the Worst by Robert Sutton (New York: Business Plus / Grand Central, 2010)

The No Asshole Rule: Building a Civilized Workplace and Surviving One That Isn't by Robert Sutton (New York: Business Plus / Grand Central, 2007)

Recommended *Harvard Business Review* Articles

"Social Intelligence and the Biology of Leadership" by Daniel Goleman and Richard Boyatzis, September 2008

"Harnessing the Science of Persuasion" by Robert B. Cialdini, October 2001

"Level 5 Leadership: The Triumph of Humility and Fierce Resolve" by Jim Collins, July–August 2005

"Connect, Then Lead: To Exert Influence You Must Balance Competence with Warmth" by Amy Cuddy, Matthew Kohut, and John Neffinger, July–August 2013

"Managing Oneself" by Peter F. Drucker, January 2005

Index

Index

Index

Hallowell, Edward, 44

health. *See also* thriving amidst incivility
  of author's father, stress and, 14–15
  exercise and, 64, 172–173
  mental, incivility and, 16
  mindfulness and, 66
  nutrition and, 65–66
  sleep and, 64–65
  stress impacting, 15–16
  taking care of yourself, 64–66

Heen, Sheila, 55

hiring. *See* recruiting and hiring

Housman, Michael, 122

IBM, 99

Implicit Association Test, 85–89, 186

incivility
  author's background and, 2–3
  brain burn from, 44–45
  bubble strategy to deal with, 43, 44–45
  civility "overwriting," 42
  civility vs., scenario options, 3–4
  correcting. *See* civility checkup;
    coaching; incivility test; practicing;
    scoring; strategies for improving
    civility
  directed at you. *See* incivility, when
    you're the target
  emotional "plague" from, 39–41
  in eyes of recipient, 10
  feelings vs. intentions, 10
  frequency of incidents, 9–10
  ignorance as basis of, 12
  labor department employee
    experience, 1–2
  lasting/recurring effects of, 44–45
  no-compromise attitude toward,
    155–157
  overview of author's perspective, 2–3
  physical reactions from, 44–45
  range of examples, 10
  shutting people down, 23, 24–25,
    38–39

  sneaking into subconscious, 41–42
  spreading of, 39–45, 46
  succeeding despite, 36
  surveys on, 9–10
  taking it seriously, 25
  terminating offenders, 158–159
  this book and, 4–5
  trends and causes, 11–13
  watching out for, 138–139

incivility, costs of, 14–25. *See also* stress
  about: overview and key points,
    7, 24–25
  bottom-line impact, 3, 16–19,
    122–123
  cognitive skills impact, 19–24
  customer dissatisfaction, 18–19
  draining managers' time, 17–18
  healthcare costs, 17
  lost sales, 18
  in medical settings, 22–23
  performance impact, 19–21, 22–23
  sidelining one from work, 20–21
  undermining altruistic behavior,
    24
  undetected losses, 17

incivility, when you're the target,
    163–176. *See also* thriving amidst
    incivility
  about: overview and key points, 163,
    176
  brain response to, 164–165
  confronting perpetrator, 165–167
  leaving work as result of, 175–176
  not getting sucked in, 165–167
  not just "sucking it up," 164–165

incivility test
  about: overview of, 50–51
  assessing, using information from,
    53–54
  guidelines for taking, 50–51
  questions to answer, 51–53
  website address, 50

innovate, opportunities to, 171–172

226

Index

Index

Index

Index